Best
Tea Shop Walks
in
South & West Wales

Dorothy Hamilton

Published by Sigma Leisure – an imprint of
Sigma Press, 1 South Oak Lane, Wilmslow, Cheshire SK9 6AR, England.

British Library Cataloguing in Publication Data
A CIP record for this book is available from the British Library.

ISBN: 1-85058-764-7

Typesetting and Design by: Sigma Press, Wilmslow, Cheshire.

Cover photographs: main picture – Tenby North Beach; smaller pictures, from top – St David's cathedral; the Pembrokshire coastal path; the Preseli Hills.
Maps: Jeremy Semmens
Photographs: Dorothy Hamilton

Printed by: MFP Design and Print

Disclaimer: the information in this book is given in good faith and is believed to be correct at the time of publication. No responsibility is accepted by either the author or publisher for errors or omissions, or for any loss or injury howsoever caused. Only you can judge your own fitness, competence and experience.

Contents

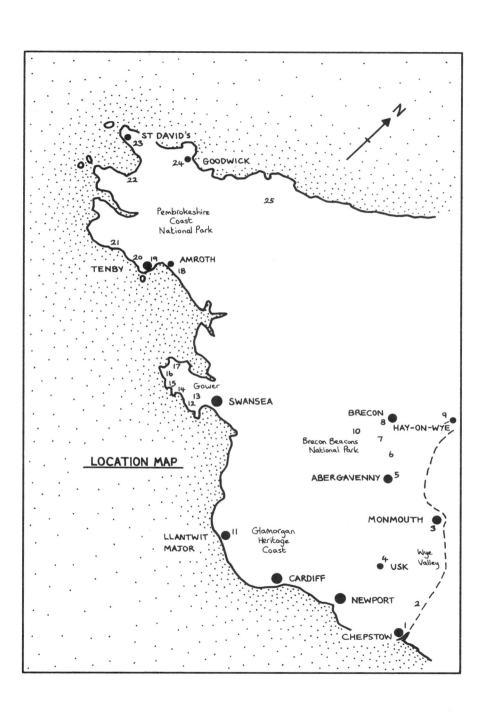

ST DAVID'S
23

24 GOODWICK

22

25

Pembrokeshire
Coast
National Park

21

20 19 AMROTH
TENBY 18

17
16
15 14 Gower
12 13 SWANSEA

LOCATION MAP

BRECON 9
8 HAY-ON-WYE
10
7
Brecon Beacons
National Park 6

ABERGAVENNY 5

MONMOUTH
3

LLANTWIT 11 Glamorgan
MAJOR Heritage
Coast

4 USK Wye
Valley

CARDIFF

NEWPORT

2

1
CHEPSTOW

Introduction

South and West Wales offer an immense variety of breathtaking scenery from valleys and gorges to moorland, mountains and coastline. With its amazing diversity of footpaths, this jigsaw of landscapes is made for the walker.

In the east corner of this area, the River Wye meanders through a deep wooded valley, evocative of monks, eccentrics and past travellers. The nearby, wider Vale of Usk has a peaceful, pastoral charm. Mountains surround the historical town of Abergavenny and some of the best views are from the Usk's meadows. A short distance away, the Monmouthshire and Brecon Canal has delightful towpath walking, full of interest. In the Brecon Beacons National Park, gentle climbs to vantage points above the valleys are rewarded by panoramic views.

Steeped in legend, the Glamorgan Heritage Coast is known for its near vertical cliffs and spectacular rock platforms. Farther west, Gower, the first designated Area of Outstanding Natural Beauty in England and Wales, is a fascinating small peninsula with a beautiful, varied coastline. In the far west, the Pembrokeshire Coast National Park boasts magnificent scenery and long stretches of cliff paths.

Wales' first visitors arrived in the Palaeolithic era when Britain was, at some stage, part of the European landmass. Several caves in Wales have yielded evidence of Stone Age man, one being the Hoyle's Mouth Cave near Tenby where many flint artefacts were found. Excavations in the Paviland Cave on Gower revealed a skeleton, minus a head, buried about 25,000 years ago. During the era known as the Neolithic period (New Stone Age) the first farmers arrived in Britain. They brought wheat, barley, sheep, goats and cattle and lived in small social groups. They left behind communal tombs and Parc le Breos on Gower is an interesting example. A small tomb of this period is seen on the walk starting at Manorbier. Burial custom changed to cremation during the Bronze Age and the ashes were placed in a pottery urn before being covered with stones (a cairn) or a mound of earth (a barrow). Another monument belonging to this period is the standing stone.

Settlements form the main evidence of occupation from about

600BC, the start of the Iron Age. Defences were now the main consideration and forts were established on hill tops and coastal promontories. Several families, though occasionally just one, lived inside an enclosure surrounded by ditches and banks. In the case of promontory forts, cliffs provided defence and only the neck of the headland needed banks and ditches. Gradually these people formed themselves into tribes, and by the time the Romans arrived there were five main tribes in Wales: the Cornovii and Deceangli in the north and east, the Ordovices in the north-west, the Demetae in the south-west and the Silures in the south-east. The Romans built a system of roads, forts and marching camps but it took about 30 years to overpower the Silures from the legionary base at Usk, and later Caerlon. Nothing remains of the Usk fortress but there are extensive remains at Caerlon, including an amphitheatre. The only known Roman town in west Wales was Moridunum (Carmarthen) and there is no evidence of a Roman road or fort farther west.

By the early 5th century, most Romans had left Britain and Wales entered what is sometimes called the Dark Ages, but what was in fact a revival of native Celtic culture. During the Roman occupation, Christianity had crept into Wales and the impact was reinforced a century or so later with the arrival of missionaries from Brittany and Ireland. They founded churches and monasteries. No buildings have survived from this era but there are a number of inscribed gravestones and memorial stones. A collection can be seen in the church at Llantwit Major.

During this period, there were occasional raids from the Irish and Vikings, but Wales gradually formed into a number of small kingdoms. Rhodri Fawr (the Great) briefly united parts of south with North Wales. His grandson Hywel Dda (the Good), who died in AD950, held a large kingdom in west Wales for a while, but he is best known for codifying the Welsh laws.

The Norman invasion of 1066 not only affected England, it also brought about a gradual change to Welsh life and landscape. The first Norman lord to enter this part of Wales was William fitz Osbern, the Earl of Hereford, who built castles at Chepstow and Monmouth. Bernard de Neufmarche conquered Brycheiniog then built a castle at Brecon. Glamorgan was invaded by Robert fitz Hamon of Glouces-ter. Rhys ap Tewdwr ruled south-west Wales but the Normans delayed their invasion of his territory until he died in 1093. They were unable to hold all of Pembrokeshire and this led to the creation of 'little England beyond Wales'. Walled towns with markets were built around the foot of the castles. Most pre-industrial towns in south Wales were originally a Norman borough. The Normans also set about reorganising the Celtic church and appointed a bishop at St David's. They also displaced the Celtic type of monasticism by establishing Benedictine monasteries,

After the Acts of Union of England and Wales, the Marcher lordships were abolished and Wales was divided into English type shires. Welsh law was replaced by English law and the language of the courts was English. Unfortunately, this had the effect of anglicising the Welsh ruling class, making them separate from most Welsh people.

Wales was an agricultural country until the coming of the Industrial Revolution. When the South Wales coalfield was exploited it brought employment to many thousands of people. Canals, railways and large ironworks were built and South Wales became a major exporter of coal. Industry has since declined, leading to an exodus of people from the valleys of the coalfield, an area now known for its industrial heritage and country parks.

The Tea Shops

Ending a walk at a tearoom or sheltered tea garden completes the enjoyment of a day out in Wales. All the teashops mentioned in this guide welcome walkers, but please be considerate and remove wet waterproofs and muddy boots.

The establishments chosen are varied and range from an old stable, a 19th century malting house, a boathouse and a former railway station to village post offices, town tea shops and a hotel tea garden. You can take tea in the close of Brecon Cathedral, or in specially designed buildings at Visitor Centres overlooking the Brecon Beacons and the Teifi Marshes.

As well as cream teas, many of the tea shops offer Welsh tea, which may include Welsh specialities such as bara brith and Welsh cakes. Most tea rooms provide home cooking, especially home-made cakes. A few close for the winter months. The majority would appreciate advance notice of the arrival of a large walking group.

The Walks

All the walks in this guide are circular. Stretching across South and West Wales, from the Wye and Usk valleys to the Brecon Beacons National Park, the Glamorgan Heritage Coast, Gower peninsula and Pembrokeshire Coast National Park, the walks explore a wide variety of spectacular countryside from riverbanks, gorges and towpaths to woodlands, downs, hill and coastal scenery. Some walks are fairly level, but most require a small amount of climbing. They range from 3 to 9 miles, and several of the longer routes have shorter alternatives. Most are suitable for families, but children must be closely supervised, especially near water, cliffs and other steep slopes. In windy weather, avoid routes using cliff paths. Allow plenty of time to complete the walks, particularly in the winter.

The directions and maps in this guidebook should be all you need to complete the walks. Ordnance Survey maps would help you to identify the features around you, and places not mentioned in the text. They are essential if you wish to make any changes to the routes. The maps referred to are No.'s 12, 13, 14, 35 and 36 from the Outdoor Leisure Series (2½ inches to a mile). These are for walks in the Wye Valley and the two National Parks. Explorer Maps, also 1:25 000 scale, No.'s 151, 152 and 164 cover walks on Gower, the Glamorgan Heritage Coast and around Usk.

Public Transport

Almost all the walks are accessible by public transport. Details are given for each walk. Free bus timetables are available at Tourist Information Centres.

Useful Phone Numbers

All Wales Public Transport System: 0870 608 2 608
Pembroke County Council's Passenger Transport Unit: 01437 764551
Abergavenny Tourist Information Centre: 01873 857588
Brecon Tourist Information Centre: 01874 622485
Chepstow Tourist Information Centre: 01291 623772
Monmouth Tourist Information Centre: 01600 713899
St David's Tourist Information Centre: 01437 720392
Swansea Tourist Information Centre: 01792 468321
Tenby Tourist Information Centre: 01834 842402

Welsh Place Names

Place names in Wales can sometimes cause problems. Learning these pronunciations will help:

A	ah
C	k (hard)
Ch	as in 'loch'
Dd	'th' as in 'the'
E	eh
F	v
Ff	f
G	as in 'go'
I	ee
Ll	say 'l', hold the tongue in this position and blow gently
O	oh
Th	as in 'through'
W	usually as in oo (cwm sounds like 'coom')
Y	as e in 'the'

The following translations will help in understanding Welsh place names. Some refer to geographical features or have historical connections:

Abaty	abbey
Aber	river
Allt	slope
Bach/fach	small
Bedd	grave
Betws	chapel or oratory
Blaen	head of valley
Braich	arm
Brenin	king
Brith	speckled
Bryn	hill
Bwa	arch
Bwlch	pass
Bychan	small
Cae	field
Caer	fort
Capel	chapel
Carn	cairn
Carreg	rock
Castell	castle
Cau	hollow
Cefn	ridge
Ceunant	gorge
Clawdd	embankment
Coch	red
Coed	woodland

Cors/gors	bog, marsh
Craig	crag
Croes	cross
Crug	hillock, mound
Cwm	valley
Cwrt	court
Dinas	fort
Dol/ddol	meadow
Drws	door
Du/ddu	black
Dwr	water
Dyffryn	valley
Eglwys	church
Esgair	ridge, mountain shoulder
Ffordd	road
Ffoss	ditch, trench
Ffridd	mountain pasture
Ffynnon	well, spring
Garth	hill, enclosure
Glan	riverbank
Glas	blue, green
Glyn	glen
Gorsaf	station
Grug	heather
Gwastad	level ground
Gwaun/waun	moor
Gwern	swamp
Gwyn	white
Gwynt	wind
Hafod	summer dwelling
Helyg	willows
Hen	old
Hendre	winter dwelling
Heol	road
Hen	old
Hendre	winter dwelling
Heol	road
Isaf	lower
Llan	church
Llethr	slope
Llyn	lake
Llys	court, palace
Maen	stone
Maes	field
Mawr/fawr	big
Melin/felin	mill
Moel/foel	hill
Mor	sea

Morfa	marsh
Mur	wall
Mynydd/fynydd	mountain
Nant	stream
Neuadd	hall
Newydd	new
Ogof	cave
Pant	hollow
Neuadd	hall
Newydd	new
Ogof	cave
Pant	hollow
Parc	park, field
Pen	head, top
Penrhyn	headland, promontory
Pentir	headland
Pentre	village
Pistyll	spout, cataract
Plas	mansion
Pont/bont	bridge
Porth	port
Pwll	pool
Rhaeadr	waterfall
Rhedyn	bracken
Rhiw	hill
Rhos	moorland
Rhyd	fort
Sarn	causeway, road
Sych	dry
Tafarn	inn
Tal	end
Tan	under
Tir	land
Tomen	mound
Traeth	beach
Tref	town
Trwyn	promontory
Twr	tower
Ty	house
Tyddyn	small farm
Uchaf	upper
Uwch	above, higher
Y/yr	the
Yn	in
Ysgol	school
Ysgubor	barn
Ystrad	valley floor

1. Chepstow

Route: This easy walk forms an introduction to walking in the Wye Valley and has some lovely views.

Distance: 4 miles.

How to get there: Chepstow is on the A48, east of Newport.

Public Transport: Trains to Chepstow. Buses from Monmouth and other nearby towns.

Start: Castle Dell car park, near Chepstow Castle.

Map: Outdoor Leisure 14.

For visitors who cross to Wales by the Severn Bridge, Chepstow is the first town over the border. The area has been a settlement for thousands of years and the Romans built a bridge upstream of the present Wye Bridge. The Welsh name for the town is Cas-Gwent and the Normans knew it as Striguil, but the name Chepstow is English, from Ceap (market) and stow (town). The dramatic castle above the River Wye was built by the Norman lord, Earl of Hereford, William fitz Osbern in 1067. In 1115, the lordship of Chepstow was given to the powerful de Clare family

The Wye Valley at Chepstow

and the castle was enlarged. In the 13th century, the castle was given extra protection on the landward side by the building of a wall known as the Portwall. Some of it stands around the edge of the car park. Entrance to the town was by the Town Gate, which was rebuilt in the 16th century. The castle held out against Owain Glyndŵr's rebellion but was surrendered to the Parliamentarians in the Civil War. The regicide Henry Marten was held prisoner in the east tower from 1660 to when he died in 1680. It became known as Marten's Tower. The Marquess of Worcester, who held the castle at the time of the Civil War, was made Duke of Beaufort in 1682. The family held the castle until 1914 when it was sold. It is now maintained by CADW.

The Tea Shop

St Mary's Tea Room with its outdoor tables is a popular refreshment stop for walkers visiting the Wye Valley. Main meals, baked potatoes, toasted sandwiches and a large selection of cakes are on offer. Open 9.00am - 4pm. Closed on Sundays. Tel: 01291 621711.

The Walk

1. From Castle Dell car park walk towards the castle. In a few metres veer left on a wide path to have the castle on your right. Walk uphill through the dell and emerge on a road.

2. Turn right along the pavement. Pass Dell Primary School on your right. At a signpost for the Wye Valley Walk, turn right. Walk through the Leisure Centre car park and, at the far end, look for a footpath that enters woodland.

3. Follow the enclosed path until it enters a wood. Bear right and descend a stepped path. It leads to a viewpoint known as The Alcove, which gives a fine view of Chepstow Castle and the Severn Bridge.

> The Alcove is one of the viewpoints laid out in the 18th century by Valentine Morris who owned the Piercefield Estate. Other imaginative names for- the viewpoints include The Chinese Seat and The Platform. In the woods, some holes are noticeable. They may have been made in the early 20th century by Dr Orville Owen who believed Francis Bacon wrote the works of Shakespeare. He

concluded that the manuscripts were hidden in watertight boxes somewhere near Chepstow. In the search, his workmen dug in the tidal mud of the River Wye, excavated the castle cellars and dug in the woods, mainly around The Grotto, which is near an Iron Age fort. They have not yet been found. At one time, it was believed the tidal waters of the River Wye could cure the bites of mad dogs and, as late as the mid-19th century, people were brought to Chepstow to be dipped in the rising river. One objection to this practice was that the madness being washed into the Wye would make the fish unfit to eat.

4. Continue on the path through the woods. In approximately one mile, the path starts to rise to Piercefield Cliffs, high above the meandering River Wye. In about 300 metres you will reach a footpath junction where there is a post with a yellow arrow. Leave the Wye Valley Path by taking the left fork. Cross a stile and bear right. Pass the ruins of a mansion on your right.

In the 18th century Piercefield Park was the home of Valentine Morris who had inherited a fortune on the death of his father. He laid out walks with viewpoints and seats on the western bank of the River Wye. He became bankrupt and, after selling the property to George Smith, he went out to the West Indies. Smith partly rebuilt the house, but it was sold in 1794 to Colonel Wood who extended and improved the three storey building. The drawing and dining rooms had Corinthian pillars of Egyptian marble, and a staircase rose to a gallery where hung tapestries with exotic designs. A carriage track linked the house with the river and Piercefield became one of the highlights of the Wye Tour. The house is now a shell. The Chepstow Racecourse bought part of Piercefield Park and the racecourse opened in 1926.

5. Pass a fence corner and maintain your direction to reach another corner close to a track. Turn left on this track to walk through Piercefield Park. On your right is Chepstow Racecourse and to the left are views of the Wye Valley cliffs.

6. On reaching a cattle grid, go through the kissing gate to the left of it and continue on the track through woodland. Ignore other

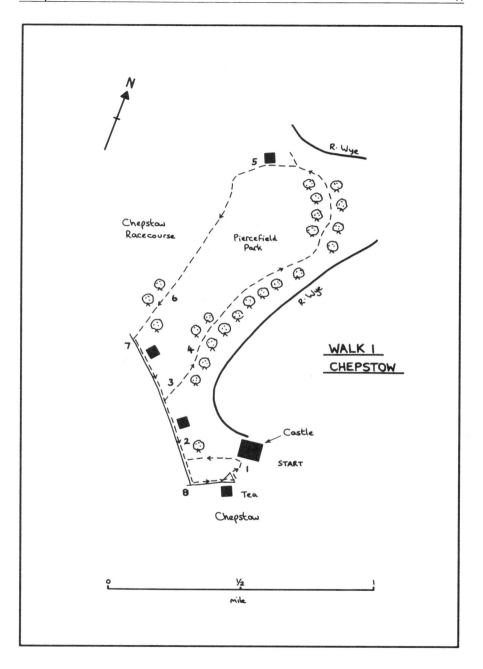

N

R· Wye

5

Chepstow
Racecourse

Piercefield
Park

R· Wye

6

WALK I
CHEPSTOW

7

4

3

2

Castle

START

1

8

Tea

Chepstow

0   ½   1
                    mile

tracks off it. When the track forks close to a high wall, bear left beside it. Go through a gap and emerge on a road.

7. Turn left and follow the road past the comprehensive school. Rejoin your outward route. Instead of returning to the start through the dell, continue along the pavement to a road junction.

8. Turn left through the Town Gate to Beaufort Square. Continue along the pedestrianised St Mary Street. St Mary's Tea Room is on your right. To return to the car park, continue along the pedestrian way to Upper Church Street. Turn left and shortly bear right down Bridge Street to Castle Dell car park and the start of the walk.

2. Tintern

Route: This delightful walk starts by following fairly level paths beside the River Wye and through woodland. After visiting Tintern Abbey, the short walk returns to the start. The alternative climbs the sides of the Angidy valley before returning to Tintern and rejoining the shorter route. Some paths may be muddy after rain.

Distance: 3¾ or 5½ miles.

How to get there: Tintern is on the A466 between Chepstow and Monmouth. Look for signs to the Old Station one mile north-east of Tintern Abbey.

Public Transport: Buses from Chepstow and Monmouth.

Start: Car park at the Old Station, Tintern. Nominal parking fee.

Map: Outdoor Leisure 14.

Before the coming of the railway, the River Wye was the main form of transport in the valley. However, the moving of goods by river was expensive and it was hoped that the opening of the railway line would ensure the survival of local industry. Construction began in 1874 and it took two years to complete the 14½ mile single line. For many years, it brought tourists to the area. Combined train and boat trips were popular, but the line was never profitable and it amalgamated with the Great Western Railway in 1905. A gradual decline in use led to it being closed to passengers in 1959. Transport of goods ceased five years later.

The Tea Shop

The Old Station Buffet is located in the former railway station. Refreshments can be taken in the restored old waiting room or outside at picnic tables. Old carriages house a railway exhibition and gift shop. Cooked meals, sandwiches and a variety of home-made cakes are on offer. Open 10.30am - 5.30pm from the beginning of April to the end of October. Tel: 01291 689566.

Whilst on the walk you may like to take refreshments at the Abbey Mill Coffee House. In the mill complex are a number of shops selling unusual arts and crafts. Lunches, cream teas and Welsh teas are on offer and there is outdoor seating. Hours 10.30am to 5.30pm (5.00pm weekdays in the winter). Open all year but closed Mondays

Tintern Old Station

and Tuesdays November to April. Check for Monday opening at other times. Tel: 01291 689228.

The Walk

1. Face the Old Station and turn right along the platform. Continue through woodland along the disused railway trackbed. At the end of the track, go up steps to the road. Turn right and cross the bridge over the River Wye to Brockweir village.

   Before the arrival of the railway, Brockweir was a small port with a shipbuilding and repair industry. Sea going ships came up the Wye to Brockweir, where the cargo was loaded into shallow barges and hauled upriver by teams of men. A ferry was the only means of crossing the river until the bridge was built in 1904. Brockweir was given its own railway halt on the north side of the river in 1929.

2. After crossing the bridge, follow the road to the right. Pass the Brockweir Inn and bear right. In approximately 20 metres, turn right at a signpost to the Brockweir Moravian church.

   The white painted Moravian church was built in 1831 on a site previously used as a cock fighting pit. At that time, Brockweir was known as a refuge for lawless persons and there was no other church here. The Moravians were a missionary body that had originated in Czechoslovakia. In the churchyard is the grave of the writer Flora Klickmann. Known for her Flower Patch books, she was also editor of The Girls Own Paper for several years. Her family came from the Wye Valley and she spent holidays at her grandparents' home near Brockweir. In 1913, her husband bought her Sylvan House nearby as a wedding present and afterwards the couple spent a lot of time at Brockweir when absent from their London home. Her Flower Patch books were inspired by the beautiful landscape of the Wye Valley. She died at the age of 92 in 1958.

3. Pass the church and bear left to a stile. Follow the path along the river bank. In approximately 300 metres veer left to a stile in the hedge. Turn right on an enclosed path and enter a wood.

Monks from Tintern Abbey used this track when they visited their farm at Brockweir. The walk passes above the old railway tunnel that emerges opposite Tintern Abbey. The northern end of the tunnel opened onto a lattice girder bridge that carried the railway line to Tintern Station.

4. Continue on a wide track through tall deciduous trees. On joining a path from the left, walk ahead downhill for views of the River Wye below. Ignore a field gate on the right. Pass a signpost and emerge on a broad track. Turn right and follow the track as it bends to the left and crosses a bridge.

The bridge is known as the wireworks bridge. Two hundred feet long, it was built in the late 19th century as a branch railway between Tintern and the Wye Valley Railway on the opposite side of the river. It also served the wire and tin plate industry in the Angidy valley.

5. Walk ahead to the A466 in Tintern. Turn left to pass Abbey Mill and turn left along a lane. In a few metres, follow the lane around to the right. When it ends, continue on a path past houses and emerge in Tintern Abbey car park.

Monks from Normandy founded the first Cistercian abbey in Wales

at Tintern in 1131 by request of the Norman lord of Chepstow
Castle. Little remains of the first buildings. The abbey was largely
rebuilt in the 13th century by another lord of Chepstow, Roger
Bigod. Although it lacks a roof and window glass, the great church
forms the most impressive part of the ruins. Tintern was the
wealthiest of the Welsh abbeys and owned several granges, plus
town property in Monmouth, Chepstow and Bristol. As well as
horses, cattle and pigs, the monks kept over 3000 sheep and
exported high quality wool to England and farther afield. After the
Dissolution the Earl of Worcester removed the lead from the abbey
and used it at Chepstow and Raglan Castles. In the late 18th
century, the Wye Valley became renowned for its picturesque
scenery and the ivy covered abbey ruins were visited by several
famous people, including William Wordsworth and J.M.W. Turner.

6. Walk out of the car park and pass the abbey ruins on your left.
(To follow the short walk, turn right along the road, and join the
longer route where it emerges on the A466 opposite Abbey Mill.)
If following the longer walk, walk straight across the main road
to a lane. Follow it uphill to a junction and turn right. In approximately 60 metres, turn left on a track. Walk along it to the ruins
of the Church of St Mary.

St Mary's Church dates from the 12th century but much
restoration work took place in 1866. A fire destroyed all but the
tower and walls in 1977. This is a lovely spot, especially in spring.

7. Continue on a narrow path to reach a signpost. Turn left and
follow a bridleway. Ignore a path on the right and, in another
200 metres, pass a house on the right. Continue along a wide
track and ignore a track and bridleway on the left.

8. Follow the main track as it bears right. Descend and pass a track
on the right to Highfield House. Ignore tracks on the left and
right and continue along the descending track. Pass a picnic
table below on the right. In another 250 metres look for a footpath and post (possibly without an arrow) on the right. Descend
to a lane and turn right for about 25 metres. Bear left and
descend an enclosed path to emerge on another lane.

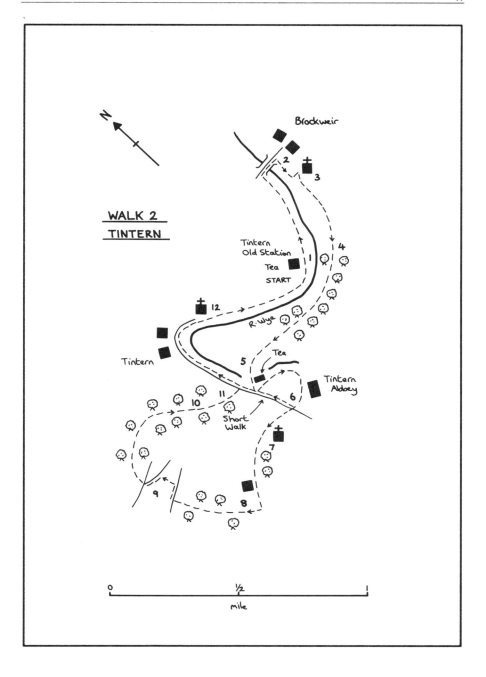

WALK 2
TINTERN

9. Turn left to follow the lane downhill to a wider lane. Cross to some steps and a railed path. On reaching a track, cross directly to another path. In about 60 metres, cross another path and continue uphill. Emerge on a wide forest track and turn right. Ignore paths left and right.

10. On reaching a point where cables cross the track, and a few metres before the track forks, veer right on a narrow path. Descend and cross a drive. Pass behind a house on a sunken path. Pass a gate to Barbados Cottage. On reaching a fork, go left. Emerge on a track and turn right to emerge on the A466 opposite Abbey Mill.

11. Walk through Tintern, with the River Wye on your right. Turn right along a lane signposted to Wye Valley Walk and St Michael's Church. Go through the churchyard to pass the church on your left.

> During the 6th century, St Tewdrig lived in a cell on the site where St Michael's Church now stands. By AD765, a Celtic church had been built here. The present church was mainly medieval prior to being restored and enlarged in 1846. It has a 13th century font and the 14th century south porch has roses on the vault.

12. Go through a small gate and emerge in a field. Follow the river bank through fields. On reaching remains of the railway bridge, leave the river by veering left through a kissing gate. Go up steps to the old railway track and turn left to follow it to the old Station, car park and Buffet.

3. Monmouth

Route: This walk gives a taste of two long distance footpaths. The Offa's Dyke Path is followed south past the Kymin, a fine viewpoint, before descending to the River Wye and a return along the Wye valley Walk to the start. Apart from one long steady climb, the route is downhill or level.

Distance: 7 miles.

How to get there: Monmouth lies south of Hereford on the A40. Plenty of car parks in the town.

Public Transport: Buses from Chepstow, Newport and Abergavenny.

Start: Shire Hall, Agincourt Square.

Map: Outdoor Leisure 14.

The ancient town of Monmouth stands at the confluence of the Rivers Wye and Monnow. It is believed to be the site of the Roman fort of Blestium, a link between Caerlon in the west and roads running north. Built in 1263,the gatehouse on the bridge over the Monnow is the only remaining one of its kind in Britain. Only fragments remain of the Norman castle founded in the late 11th century by William fitz Osbern to guard the crossings of the two rivers. He also founded a Benedictine priory where St Mary's Church is now. Henry V was born in the castle on 9 August 1387. During the Civil Wars, it changed hands several times. In 1673, the first Duke of Beaufort built the Great Castle House with the stones from the first castle. In 1875, it became the headquarters of the Royal Monmouthshire Engineer Militia. A statue of Henry V is in the wall of the Shire Hall in Agincourt Square.

The Tea Shop

On this walk you have the option of a tea garden en route and/or a coffee shop at the end of the walk.

The Maltsters Coffee Shop in St Mary Street, Monmouth is so named because it is part of a 19th century malting house. Home-made soup, Welsh rarebit, toasties, jacket potatoes and salads are on offer as well as a wide selection of cakes. Open 9.00am - 5.00pm weekdays and Saturdays. 11.00am - 4.30pm Sundays and bank holiday Mondays. Tel: 01600 713999.

The Incline Bridge Tea Garden is passed on the walk in Upper

Redbrook. Cream teas and home baked cakes are on offer. You can also eat your own sandwiches in the tea garden if you buy a pot of tea! Tel: 01600 713863.

The Walk

1. With your back to the Shire Hall, turn right. In a few metres, where the road veers left, continue along the pedestrianised Church Street. On reaching another road, turn right along St Mary's Street to where it joins St James' Street. Bear left and, in a few metres, turn right into Wyebridge Street. Use the subway on the left to pass under the A40.

2. On leaving the subway, bear right then left to cross the Wye bridge. In approximately 200 metres, where the road bears right, walk ahead on the A4136. Pass the May Hill Hotel on your right and walk uphill along the right-hand pavement. Ignore a path and steps on the right. When the pavement ends, continue on a railed path beside the road. It rises gradually and goes through two gates to emerge on a track. Turn left and, on meeting a lane, walk ahead, uphill.

3. When the lane bends sharp right, go ahead over a stile into woodland. Follow the main path uphill through tall deciduous trees. In about 250 metres, at a point where the path bears left, cross a stile on the right. Walk uphill keeping, at first, to the left side of the field. Cross a stile in the top right-hand corner.

4. Turn left along the lane and, in a few paces, go through a small gate on the left. Walk ahead uphill through woodland. In approximately 200 metres, at the end of the right-hand fence, veer right to cross the banking. Immediately go left on a path that rises to a signpost. Bear right to the Kymin.

> From Kymin hill there are extensive views of the surrounding countryside and in clear weather it is possible to see the Sugar Loaf and Ysgyryd Fawr near Abergavenny. The Banqueting House on the hill was built in 1794 as a dining club. The nearby Temple was built a few years later to celebrate the British Navy. It was visited by Nelson, who sailed up the Wye to Monmouth in July 1802. He

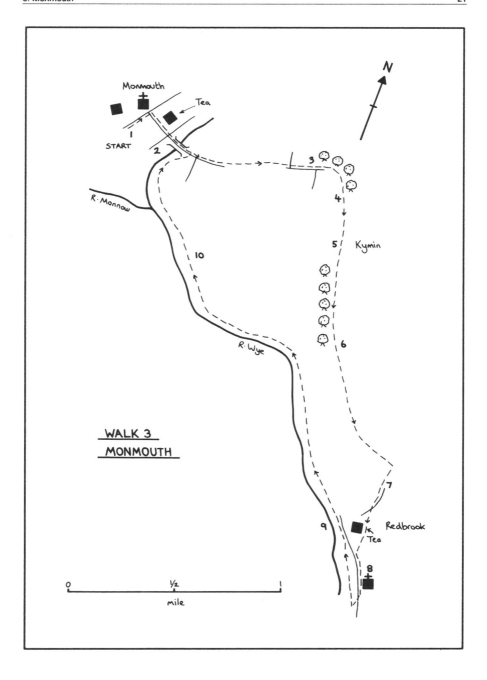

N

Monmouth

Tea

START

1

2

R. Monnow

3

4

5 Kymin

10

R. Wye

6

WALK 3
MONMOUTH

7

9

Redbrook

Tea

8

0   ½
mile

thought the Kymin was one of the most beautiful places he had ever seen.

Kymin Tower

5. After passing Kymin Tower, and the Temple, walk downhill to the National Trust parking area. Look on the left for a kissing gate and follow the path through woodland. Go through a kissing gate into a field and follow a clear path downhill beside the right boundary. Cross a stile in the right corner and continue between fences to have a field on the left and a wood on the right. Cross a stile and walk across a field on a fairly level path to another stile. Continue ahead but before reaching the corner of the field, cross a stile on the right.

6. Bear left to pass a house on your right. Join a track coming from the house and follow it downhill. After passing a farm, the track becomes steeper. Ignore paths leading off.

7. On reaching a road, bear right and in approximately 300 metres, a few paces before a bridge is above the road, veer left on a track. Pass the Incline Bridge Tea Garden and follow the track between houses to the A466.

8. Turn left on the pavement and pass a church on the left. Shortly

bear right across Redbrook Millennium Green to the River Wye. Turn right on a path and ignore a bridge on the left that leads to the Boat Inn. The route now follows the Wye Valley Walk. In a few metres, a stepped path goes down to the riverbank. In summer, the path can be rather overgrown. It eventually emerges on the A466.

9. Turn left for about 200 metres. Look for a grassy path on the left and follow it to a stile. Walk along a clear path close to the River Wye. After about 1½ miles it passes a sewage works.

10. Pass the remains of a viaduct and go under an old railway bridge. Walk along the edge of a playing-field and emerge on a road. Cross the road with care and turn left over the Wye Bridge. Use the subway to go under the A40. Walk up Wyebridge Street to the junction. Turn left along St James' Street then right along St Mary's Street to retrace your steps to the coffee shop and Agincourt Square.

4. Usk

Route: A walk in unspoilt countryside following a bridleway and paths through fields and woodland. There are lovely views throughout most of the route, which has some uphill sections.

Distance: 4 miles.

How to get there: Usk is on the A472 off the A449, north of Newport. Signposted car park in the town.

Public Transport: Buses from Monmouth and Newport.

Start: Bridge Street, Usk.

Map: Explorer 152.

Named after its river, Usk is famous for its gorgeous floral displays and regularly wins 'in Bloom' awards. The town stands on the site of a large Roman legionary base called Burrium, which controlled the area for about twenty years until Isca at Caerlon was founded in AD75. The ruined medieval castle on the hill above the town is privately owned and is not usually open to the public. The Normans built a wooden fortress here, which was replaced by stone buildings in the 12th century when the surrounding area was under the control of the de Clare family. Further additions took place in the following centuries and it became a major stronghold. After the Civil War, the castle was dismantled. Originally built for a Benedictine priory of nuns, the Church of St Mary has some interesting features.

The Tea Shop

Café en Fleur is in Bridge Street, not far from the river. The varied menu includes soup, baked potatoes, lunches, sandwiches, afternoon teas and a delicious selection of cakes. Open every day 8.30am - 5.30pm. Tel: 01291 672669.

The Walk

1. Walk away from the town centre and cross the bridge over the River Usk. Turn right and, in a few metres, bear left on a track to walk between houses. Continue between hedges and enter a field. Walk ahead to a stile at the edge of woodland. Follow a

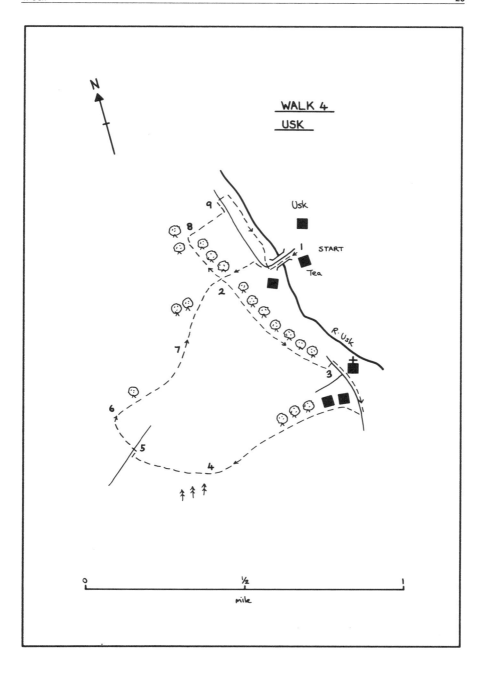

N

WALK 4
USK

Usk

START

Tea

R. Usk

9

8

1

2

7

3

6

5

4

0   ½   1
mile

path that slants to the right, uphill. Cross a stile and go up steps to another.

2. Turn left along the edge of the field. Cross a stile into the next field and continue beside the left-hand fence. Cross another corner stile and maintain your direction to the end of the field. Cross a stile beside a gate and walk downhill on a sunken path. Pass some buildings and in about 20 metres bear left on a waymarked footpath. Descend to a road and turn right.

3. Pass a lane on the right and in another 100 metres turn right on a track. After Ty Mawr Farm the track bends right and, shortly, left to pass some houses on the right. Walk ahead on a steep path that rises into woodland. Cross a stile and continue ahead to pass between fields.

4. Descend to a small gate and follow an enclosed way to another gate and stile. Continue on a clear track. Pass a wood on the left and enter a field. Walk ahead downhill and veer to the right to follow a line of bushes and trees towards the valley. Go through a gate and emerge on a lane.

5. Turn right and, in a few metres, go through a field gate on the left. Walk ahead and in about 100 metres look for a yellow arrow in the trees on the right. Cross a small footbridge over a stream and veer right to a stile. Follow a path uphill through trees to another stile.

6. Turn left on a track and, in a few paces, cross a stile on the right. Walk across the field to the next stile, which is at the edge of some trees. Follow the left boundary of the field. On reaching the corner, cross a stile on the left. Slant to the right and walk uphill. Pass a fenced off area and cross the middle of the field to a stile in the hedge.

7. Cross this field to a stile near a gate. Walk ahead to another stile and cross the next field to reach the stile at the woodland edge, i.e. the stile crossed earlier on the walk. Do not cross but bear left along the edge of the field beside the wood. In about 100 metres

climb a stile to enter the wood. Walk downhill and, at a waymarked post, bear right.

8. In about 30 metres, at another post, veer left and shortly cross a small footbridge over a stream. Ignore a stile on the left and bear right. Pass a footbridge on the right and continue ahead beside trees. Go through a gate and walk ahead on a track to emerge on the A472.

9. Cross the road with care and turn left for about 100 metres. Bear right into 'The Island' car park and go up steps to the parkland. Turn right to have the River Usk on your left. Pass a children's playground and continue on a path above the river. Go up steps to the road and bear left. Cross the bridge over the River Usk and retrace your steps to the start of the walk.

A quiet afternoon in the town of Usk

5. Abergavenny

Route: A superb, varied walk taking in riverside, canal and woodland paths as well as a stroll along the side of Blorenge mountain. There is one steady climb of about 1000 feet, which is rewarded by beautiful views of the surrounding countryside.

Distance: 8 miles.

How to get there: Abergavenny is on the A40 between Brecon and Monmouth.

Public Transport: Trains to Abergavenny. Buses from Brecon, Newport and Monmouth.

Start: Car park near the Tourist Information Centre and Bus Station on the A40 in Abergavenny.

Map: Outdoor Leisure 13.

Surrounded by hills, the pleasant market town of Abergavenny lies at the confluence of the little Gavenny river with the Usk. To the north rises the cone of the Sugar Loaf, whilst across the Usk is the massive bulk of Blorenge. North-east is Ysgryd Fawr with a ruined chapel on its summit

Blorenge

whilst directly east is the lower wooded Ysgryd Fach. The Romans had a fort here, Gobannium. Shortly after the Norman invasion in the 11th century, Hamelin de Balun built a motte and bailey castle. More building took place in the following centuries but only fragments remain. The castle is remembered for the treachery of William de Braose who, in 1175, invited the local chieftain Seisyllt ap Dyfnwal and other local people to a banquet on Christmas Day. Whilst they feasted, de Braose and his men slaughtered them in revenge for the death of Lord Henry of Hereford, de Braose's uncle. His men went to the chieftain's castle and killed his young son, Cadwaladr. Five years later the Welsh burnt the Norman castle. William de Braose survived but thirty years later he was left a beggar when King John took away his land. The burial place of several Marcher lords, St Mary's Church contains some fine medieval monuments and a wooden figure of Jesse.

The Tea Shop

Chat's Café in Cross Street serves main meals, jacket potatoes, salads, apple pie, scones and a delicious selection of cakes. There is also a tea garden. Open daily, usually 7.00am - 5.00pm. On Sundays, it opens at 9.00am.

The Walk

1. From the Tourist Information Centre, turn right. Ignore Mill Street on the left and continue approximately another 100 metres then turn left along Castle Street. When the road turns right, bear left on a lane signposted to Castle and Museum. Pass the castle grounds on the left and, at the end of the lane, continue on a path that descends to a kissing gate. Walk ahead through Castle Meadows to the River Usk. From here, you have fine views of the surrounding hills, especially Blorenge to the south-west.

2. Turn right along the riverside path. On meeting a road, turn left across the bridge then immediately take a lane on the right signposted to Llanfoist cemetery. Walk along the lane and follow it when it bears left to pass under the A465. When the lane ends at a nursery, continue ahead on the track signposted as a cycle route.

3. After passing a playing field on the left and a disused railway line on the right (used on the return route), cross a road and continue ahead on a lane. Pass Llanfoist Parish Church on your left. Follow this shady lane uphill. When it veers left to a gate and drive leading to The Boathouse, turn right on a path. On reaching a signpost, go left and walk through a tunnel that passes under the Monmouthshire and Brecon Canal to emerge on the drive near The Boathouse.

4. Cross directly to a stile at the edge of woodland. Ignore a path on the left and walk ahead uphill on the main path to follow a stream on the left. Cross a stile and, in a few metres, a track and continue along the path, uphill. After crossing another stile, walk beside a fence on your right. On reaching a track, where there is a gate on the right, go ahead uphill. Ignore a stile on the right, but continue uphill to a stile in the fence ahead. Look back for fine views of the Sugar Loaf.

5. Continue uphill a few metres to join a clear path. Turn right and follow it along the open hillside below the summit of Blorenge. The path runs slightly above a fence. On reaching a fork, ignore the left-hand path that goes uphill. Continue on a path above a fence and, in places, a wall. It was once a tramroad for the iron industry.

6. About 100 metres before the path meets the forest, and at a point where the fence bears right away from the path, turn right to follow a narrow path beside the fence. Go downhill to a stile at the edge of the forest. Follow a clear path, waymarked with yellow arrows, through the coniferous trees. Cross a stile to emerge on a road.

7. Cross the road directly to a rather rough, stony path on the opposite side. Within 60 metres, it becomes a narrow, shady path descending between fields. Emerge on a lane and turn right. Ignore a lane on the right. In about 50 metres, leave the lane as it bears right and cross an old bridge. Bear right and, in 200 metres, pass a road on the right.

8. In a few metres you will reach the Monmouthshire and Brecon

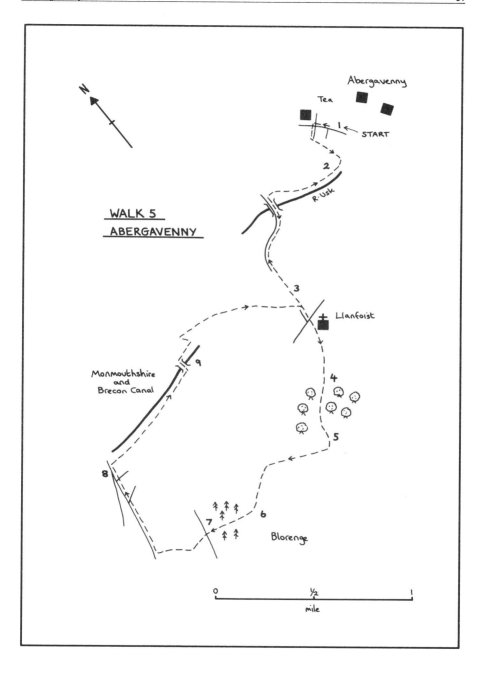

WALK 5
ABERGAVENNY

Canal. Do not cross the bridge but turn right to walk along the towpath with the canal on your left. Pass the moorings of the Govilon Boat Club and pass under a road bridge. The towpath runs alongside woods and ends on this side of the canal. Cross a bridge and bear right to have the canal on your right.

9. Shortly, leave the canal to bear left on a path that descends to the cycle path along the old railway line. Turn right and follow the track to its end near the road at Llanfoist. Bear left on the lane and retrace your outward route past the playing field, under the A465 and on through Castle Meadows. After walking down Castle Street, and emerging at Cross Street, turn left. Chat's Café is on the right-hand side.

6. Crickhowell

Route: Canal and field paths are followed on this easy, almost completely flat, walk which has several interesting features and lovely views.

Distance: 3¾ miles.

How to get there: Crickhowell is on the A40, north-west of Abergavenny.

Public Transport: Buses from Abergavenny and Brecon.

Start: High Street, Crickhowell.

Map: Outdoor Leisure 13.

Crickhowell lies on the east side of the River Usk, which is spanned by a 17th century 13 arch bridge. The small town takes its name from Crug Hywel (Hywel's Mound), a distinctive flat topped hill situated to the north. Capped by an Iron Age fort, the hill is also known as Table Mountain. The remains of Crickhowell Castle can be found in the town's park. Originally built in the 12th century by the Turberville family, the motte and bailey castle was rebuilt in stone about 1272 by Sir Grimbald Pauncefote who married a Turberville. Only fragments of a tower and wall are still standing. During Owain Glyndŵr's rebellion the castle was destroyed. Sir George Everest, who was born in 1790 at the nearby Gwernvale House (now called Manor Hotel), was a surveyor in India and Mount Everest was named after him. He is buried in the graveyard of Crickhowell church.

The Tea Shop

The Cheese Press Coffee Shop is cosily located at the rear of the gift shop in the cheese press building. The menu includes main meals, salads, toasted sandwiches and a delectable selection of home-made cakes, including fudge cake. Open Mondays, Tuesdays, Thursdays, Fridays and Saturdays from 9.30am - 4.30pm. Wednesdays 9.30am - 1.00pm. Sundays 11.00am - 4.30pm. Tel: 01873 811122.

The Walk

1. Walk along the High Street and pass The Cheese Press on your right. On reaching a fork, bear right down Bridge Street. Cross the bridge over the River Usk and turn right in the direction of Talybont-on-Usk.

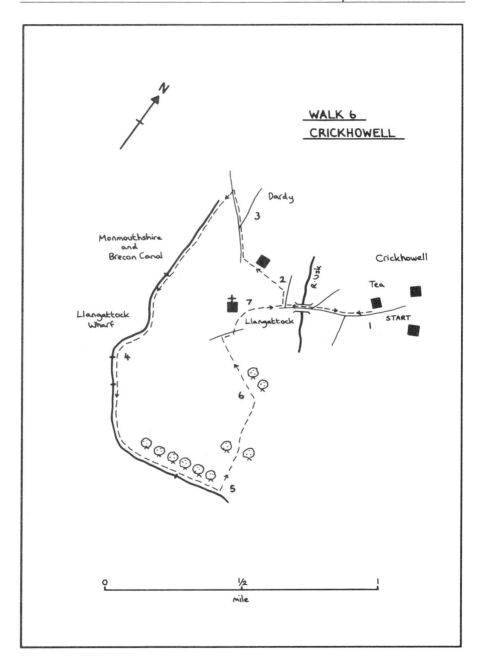

2.   In approximately 70 metres bear left through a kissing gate. Follow the clear path ahead as it slants slightly to the right. At the end of the field, follow the hedge on the left to a kissing gate. Pass a barn on the left and join a drive coming from Cwrt Isaf Farm. Walk uphill along the drive to a lane.

3.   Turn right and in 350 metres at Dardy, bear left to go up a steep lane. A few metres before reaching a bridge that crosses the Monmouthshire and Brecon Canal, bear left to join the towpath. Turn left to walk with the canal on your right. To your left are views of the flat topped Table Mountain. Pass under a road bridge and in another 600 metres you will arrive at Llangattock Wharf.

> On the west side of the canal at Llangattock Wharf are lime kilns and the wharfinger's house, which was built in 1800 by the canal company. A horsedrawn tramway brought limestone from the quarries (now abandoned) high above on Mynydd Llangatwg. The canal was originally two canals – the Monmouthshire Canal and the Brecknock and Abergavenny Canal. They joined end to end at Pontypool. The complete route from Brecon to Newport opened in 1812. Limestone, coal and iron ore were transported to the south

Llangattock Wharf

Wales iron industries or exported from the docks at Newport. After the coming of the railways, trade declined and the canal became derelict. It has now been restored for use by recreational boats and walkers.

4. Go under the road bridge and pass more moorings. After another bridge, continue along the tree lined canal. Pass under one more bridge and continue with a wall on the left. When the wood on your left ends, and a few metres before a bridge between fields, cross a stile on your left.

5. Walk ahead to join a track coming from the bridge. Go left to follow a fence. When the track bends left, cross a stile and descend a clear path through coniferous woodland. Go down to a stile and walk straight across a long field. Go through a kissing gate near the left-hand corner and emerge on a track. Turn right and cross a stream. On your right is Llangattock Beech Wood.

6. Continue along the metalled track to pass the wood on your right. On reaching a road junction in Llangattock, turn right. In approximately 50 metres, before the road bends right, turn left along a path between buildings. It bears right to a kissing gate. Follow the paved path ahead. In about 30 metres go through the kissing gate on the left if you wish to visit Llangattock church.

Llangattock church is dedicated to St Cattwg, also known as St Cadoc, who lived in the 6th century. The son of St Gwynlliw, King of Gwent, and St Gwladys, daughter of King Brychan, he was educated at Llanilltud Fawr (Llantwit Major) and travelled to Ireland and Brittany. He was a contemporary of St David. As well as founding several churches he set up a monastery at Llancarfan in Glamorgan, which became an important centre for learning. The oldest part of Llangattock church is the 12th century tower. There are some interesting monuments.

7. Continuing on the walk, follow the paved path to a kissing gate. Walk ahead and emerge on the B4558. Cross carefully and retrace your steps over the bridge-. Walk up Bridge Street to 'The Cheese Press' and the start of the walk.

7. Talybont-on-Usk

Route: This interesting, varied walk may be slightly strenuous, but it offers superb views over the surrounding countryside. Easy towpath walking is followed by hillside, woodland and riverside paths.

Distance: 7 miles.

How to get there: Leave the A40 2 miles east of Brecon to follow the B4558 to Talybont-on-Usk. Car parking space across the drawbridge.

Start: The Drawbridge Coffee Shop and Tea Room in Talybont-on-Usk.

Maps: Outdoor Leisure 12 and 13.

The Monmouthshire and Brecon Canal passes through the pretty village of Talybont-on-Usk on its placid journey from Brecon to Newport. The northern section was constructed as the Brecknock and Abergavenny Canal for carrying iron ore from the mines in the mountains. In the mid-19th century, the Monmouthshire Canal and Railway Company purchased this stretch and the canal system from Brecon to Newport became the Monmouthshire and Brecon Canal.

Countryside around Talybont-on-Usk

The Tea Shop

The Drawbridge Coffee Shop and Tea Room is located opposite the canal in Talybont. Breakfasts, light lunches, afternoon teas and a good selection of cakes are on offer. There are tables outside. Open every day 9.00am - 5.30pm from Easter to the end of September. Tel: 01874 676663.

The Walk

1.   On the opposite side of the road to the Drawbridge Coffee Shop and Tea Room, follow a zigzag path up to the Monmouthshire and Brecon Canal. Turn right to pass the drawbridge and, with the canal on your left, follow the towpath. In about two miles you will pass the site of Pencelli Castle.

   A mound is all that remains of the Norman Castle of Pencelli. The original owner is unknown but at one time it was held by Gwladis, the daughter of Llywelyn ap Iorwerth (the Great), who had married Reginald de Breos. By second marriage, it passed to the Mortimers. Adjoining the site, a Tudor manor house built by the Herberts is known as Pencelli Castle.

2.   Go under a road bridge at Pencelli. Pass some gardens and, at the next bridge, leave the towpath. Bear left over the bridge to a road. Bear right and ignore a stile on the left. Turn left on a lane signposted to Llanfeugan church. Pass Pencelli Outdoor Education Centre on the right and walk uphill. Pass a parking area. In a few metres turn left on a track – but continue along the lane a few metres if you wish to see Llanfeugan church.

   Llanfeugan church was founded by St Meugan, who lived in the 7th century. It is believed he, and other missionaries, came from Caerleon and built a wooden church on this spot. The Lord of Pencelli built a stone church here in the 13th century. The windows and doorway in the north wall are of that date. Enlargements and alterations took place early in the 15th century when the tower was built and extensive restoration was carried out 400 years later. A tragedy befell the parish in 1753 when a wedding party – including bride and groom – on their way to the church drowned in the

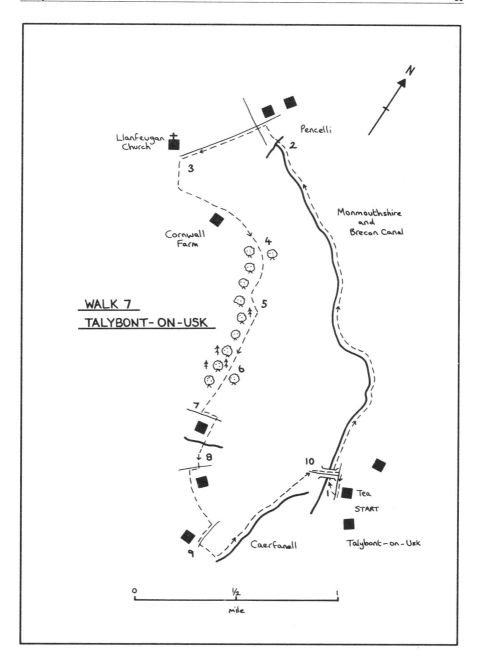

Pencelli

Llanfeugan
Church

Monmouthshire
and
Brecon Canal

Cornwall
Farm

WALK 7
TALYBONT- ON-USK

Tea

START

Caerfanell

Talybont-on-Usk

0   ½   1
                   mile

flooded River Usk. Their graves are in the churchyard. The yew trees at the eastern end of the churchyard are thought to be at least 2000 years old. Only the shaft remains of the old preaching cross which the Puritans destroyed in the 17th century.

3. Follow the enclosed track. After passing through a gate it reaches a junction. Turn left and, farther on, ignore a stile on the left. Walk between the buildings of Cornwall Farm and continue ahead. Go through a gate across the track and, in a few paces, bear right over a stile. Ignore a stile on the left signed Lower Cross Oak.

4. Follow the track uphill (signposted to Coity Mawr). It bears left to reach the edge of woodland. Continue on the main track through trees. Emerging from the trees, the track bears a little right to continue uphill. Cross a stile near a gate and, a little farther on, stay on the track when it bears right. In about 40 metres, turn left on a narrow path which passes a small ruin on its right. On reaching a fence, cross a stile to emerge in a field.

5. Walk along the hillside to have a fence on the right. When there is a fence ahead, bear right to a stile. Follow the path through trees and, after crossing a stream, climb a stile into a coniferous wood. Descend to another stile and bear right. After crossing a stream and stile, follow a fence through deciduous trees.

6. Emerge in a field and walk ahead. After descending into a dip, follow the right-hand fence uphill to a stile. Walk ahead to pass trees nearby on the left. Continue between fences to a stile at a gate. Walk beside the left-hand fence to pass Coity Mawr, which is below on the left. At the bottom of the field, bear left to a stile at a gate.

7. Bear left to walk along the lane. In about 30 metres, cross a stile on the right. Walk downhill alongside trees. Cross a stile and descend the stepped path to another stile. Bear right to cross a footbridge and ascend the stepped path to a field. Follow the right-hand boundary to a stile and lane.

8. Turn right to walk uphill along the lane. In approximately 50

metres, bear left over a stile. Pass above a farmhouse and cross a stile to the left of a gate. Continue ahead along the right side of the field to the next stile. Now, slant left downhill to the bottom left corner of the field. Follow an old track to a broad gate. Turn right along the lane.

9. On reaching a farmhouse on the right, cross a stile on the left. Walk downhill and veer left to a stile at the bottom of the field. Walk beside the Caerfanell and ignore a footbridge across it. Go through a kissing gate and walk ahead to rejoin the river bank. Cross a stile and continue beside trees. In 100 metres leave the river to bear slightly left to a stone stile.

10. Bear right along the lane. In approximately 300 metres, pass a parking space on the left. Cross the drawbridge and bear right to reach the start of the walk at the Drawbridge Coffee Shop and Tea Room.

8. Brecon

Route: A woodland path beside and above the Honddu River leads to quiet lanes and a climb to Pen-y-crug hill fort before descending past a holy well and Brecon Cathedral. Some paths could be muddy and slippery after rain.

Distance: 5½ miles.

How to get there: Brecon lies off the A40, between Abergavenny and Llandovery.

Public Transport: Buses from Hereford, Abergavenny, Swansea, Merthyr Tydfil and Llandrindod Wells.

Start: Signposted car park near the Tourist Information Centre.

Map: Outdoor Leisure 12.

Today, Brecon is a busy market town. Settlement goes back to the Iron Age when the summit of Pen-y-crug was fortified. The Romans built a fort a few miles west, in about AD75, with roads to Cardiff and Neath. The name Brecon is thought to be derived from Brycheiniog, the kingdom of Brychan, a 5th century prince of Irish ancestry. Brecon itself was founded when, in 1091 the Norman lord Bernard de Neufmarche, a half-brother of William the Conqueror, marched from Herefordshire into the area and built a castle between the Usk and Honddu rivers. In the 18th century, Brecon was a fashionable place for rich people to overwinter. There are a number of fine Georgian and Victorian buildings.

The Tea Shop

The Pilgrims Tea Rooms makes a fitting end to this walk, which may have taken in a visit to the cathedral itself. The tea shop is situated in the cathedral close and there are tables outside in the herb garden. Only local produce is used and this includes organic salads. The menu offers a choice of teas: cream tea, pilgrim's tea and Welsh tea. The last includes Caerphilly cheese, bara brith and Welsh cake. Open seven days a week 10.30am to 4.30pm. Tel: 01874 610610.

The Walk

1.   With your back to the Tourist Information Centre, turn right and

The Brecon Beacons

walk out to the road. Bear left downhill to a junction. Turn right and ignore a road called Priory Hill on the left. In another 50 metres look for a footbridge on your left. Cross the River Honddu and bear right.

2. In a few metres, veer right on a woodland path through Priory Groves. It runs parallel to the river. Ignore a path going uphill but go ahead and pass through a kissing gate. Cross a meadow and enter woodland. Climb to where the path forks and go left on the higher path to reach a path junction. Turn right and, at a fork, take the left-hand path in the direction of Anod Bridge.

3. With a field on the left, walk ahead. In about 400 metres, at a wooden signpost, look for a footbridge on the right. Descend to cross the stream and climb steps. Go through the woods to reach the field edge again. Continue on a narrow path to a stile. Bear right downhill towards the river and walk ahead through the field to a stile.

4. Turn left along the quiet lane to the B4520. Turn right along the grass verge and ignore a lane on the right. Take the first road on

the left, signposted to Cradoc. In 600 metres, about 60m before the top of a rise, turn left on a track.

5. Follow the enclosed grassy track to a gate giving access to an open hillside. Go ahead on a clear path that has a bridleway (blue) sign. In approximately 400 metres, the path forks. To reach the top of the hill, take the right-hand path. It passes through the ditches of Pen-y-crug fort, before rising to the summit.

    Pen-y-crug Iron Age hill fort occupies the summit of a hill which overlooks the Usk and Honddu valleys. The fort was strongly defended by three, in places four, banks and ditches. There is an entrance on the south-east side. From the summit are fine views of Brecon and the Beacons.

6. Leave the summit by taking a path that leads towards the left side of Brecon. Ignore paths going off to the right. Follow the path to a waymarked post on the bridleway and immediately leave it by taking a path on the right. Where the path bends left, ignore paths on the right. Follow the main path to a stile near trees.

7. Walk ahead, downhill, through the field to a stile left of the right-hand corner. The next stile is in view ahead. Continue walking ahead and after crossing the last stile, where there is woodland on the left, bear left a few paces to see Maen-du well.

    Maen-du holy well is covered by a Celtic type stone building that was rebuilt in 1754. The well was visited by lovers who threw pins into the water before making a wish.

8. Return to the main path and walk out to a small parking area. Bear left on the wide grass verge and pass timber clad houses. On reaching a road junction, bear right along the pavement. Continue downhill and pass the entrance gates to the Cathedral and Cathedral Close on your left.

    Bernard de Neufmarche founded a Benedictine monastery here in 1093. The Benedictines permitted their churches to be used by the parish, therefore at the Dissolution of the Monasteries the church

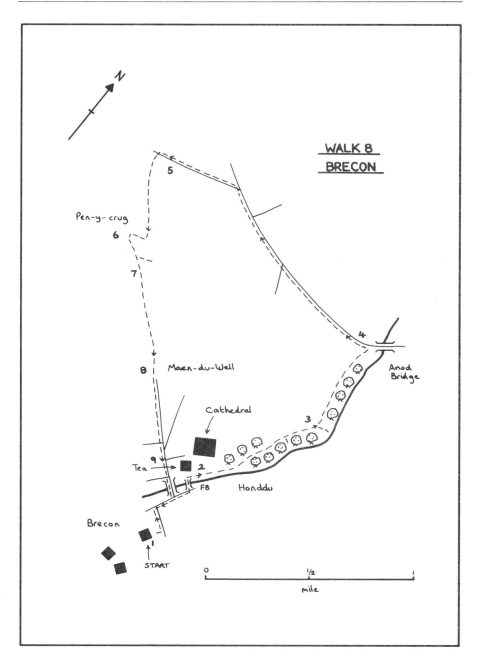

WALK 8
BRECON

survived, unlike those belonging to the Cistercians. The Church of St John was a parish church until 1923 when it became the cathedral of the new diocese of Swansea and Brecon. The building dates mainly from the 13th and 14th centuries. Near the door, the 12th century font survives from an earlier church. In the north aisle is the ancient Guild Chapel of Shoemakers. The story of the cathedral is told in the Heritage Centre (admission free) which is in Cathedral Close.

9. Follow the road down Priory Hill to a junction. Turn right, then left, to retrace your steps to the start at the car park.

9. Hay-on-Wye

Route: A gentle, ascending route following the Offa's Dyke Path is followed by lesser known paths with wide views of the surrounding countryside. Some paths could be muddy after rain.

Distance: 5 miles.

How to get there: Hay-on-Wye lies north-east of Brecon and west of Hereford. Take the A438 to Clyro then the B4351.

Public Transport: Buses from Brecon and Hereford.

Start: Signposted car park near the Tourist Information Centre.

Map: Outdoor Leisure 13.

Hay-on-Wye is famous throughout the world as a town of second-hand bookshops. There are over 30 of them! It all started in 1961 when Richard Booth of Hay Castle opened a shop to sell second-hand books. His dream of establishing the largest second-hand book centre in the world has been fulfilled. The town's history goes back to the early 12th century when the Normans built a motte and bailey castle here. Hay's name is

Above Hay-on-Wye

from the Norman 'la haie', meaning 'the wood'. A stone castle was built by the notorious William de Braose who murdered the Welsh chieftain Seisyllt and his young son Cadwaladr. Some say the castle was built by his wife Maud de St Valery (better known as Moll Wallbee) and it was she who accused King John of murdering his nephew, Arthur of Brittany. She and one of her sons were imprisoned and starved to death in Windsor or Corfe Castle. Her husband escaped to France. The castle and town walls were destroyed by fire during Owain Glyndŵr's rebellion. In the early 17th century, the Gwynn family built the Jacobean mansion inside the Norman walls. Since then, the castle has seen a variety of tenants and owners. The cleric and diarist Francis Kilvert of Clyro was a frequent visitor to the castle in the 1870s.

The Tea Shop

Known for its relaxed atmosphere, The Granary in Broad Street is a popular restaurant and café with pavement tables, from where it is very pleasant to watch the world go by in this little town of books. The extensive menu includes main meals, salads, baked potatoes, scones and cream, and delicious apple pies. Open every day except Christmas Day and Boxing Day. Usual hours 10.00am to 9.00pm, except in the winter when closing time is earlier. Check at other times if likely to be arriving late. Tel: 01497 820790.

The Walk

1. From the car park, turn right and, in a few metres, bear right on a track to follow the Offa's Dyke Path. When the track ends, go through the second kissing gate and walk ahead with a hedge on the left. Ignore a stile on the left. Go through another kissing gate and follow a fence on the right to the next gate. Continue ahead, passing through another gate, and cross a footbridge.

2. Walk uphill and cross a stile. Follow the left-hand fence to the next stile. Walk ahead for about 40 metres then cross the field diagonally right to a stile located a short distance before the far corner.

3. Turn left and walk along the lane. In 600 metres, cross a stile on the right and walk ahead to follow a line of trees on your right. In

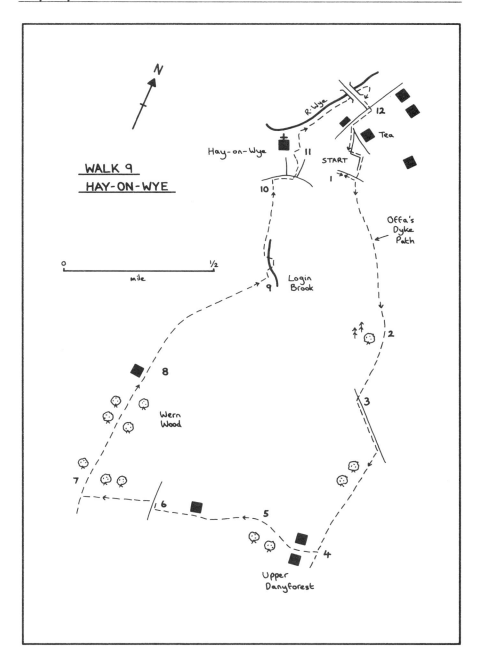

WALK 9
HAY-ON-WYE

approximately 200 metres, opposite a house on the left, and before the end of the field, bear right to cross a footbridge and stile. Follow the left boundary of this field to another stile. Continue ahead on a clear path.

4. Emerge on the access lane to Upper Danyforest. Turn right and pass the house on your left. Pass buildings on the right and go through a gate. In a few paces, go through a gate on the right and follow the left boundary of the field to a stile. Walk ahead, bearing slightly right, on a path through trees. Cross a stile and walk ahead through the field to the next stile.

5. Descend to cross a stream and go up to another stile. Cross this field by bearing slightly right to the next stile and field. Maintain your direction to go through a gate and emerge on a farm track. Bear right through a gate into the farmyard. Go left into another field and follow the right boundary to a stile.

6. Turn right along the lane but, in a few paces, cross a stile in the hedge on the left. Cross the field well above the trees, which lie below, on your right. From this point there are superb views across the valley. Go through a field gate at a point where an old grassy track on the left reaches it. Turn right beside the fence on your right and cross a stile at the edge of trees.

7. Follow a clear path through the trees and emerge in a clearing. Cross (being careful not to descend to the right) to find a clear path through more trees. After another grassy stretch enter Wern Wood on a wide path. Emerge in a field and pass a ruin on the left.

8. Cross a stile near a gate and walk ahead to the next stile and gate. Go ahead, slanting to the left, through the middle of the field in the direction of a distant farm. On reaching the left-hand hedge, follow it downhill into a clearing. Continue ahead to another field. Follow the right-hand boundary of this field, which narrows. Continue on a path, which becomes a track bordered by trees.

9. On reaching a field gate ahead, go through a small gate below it

on the left. Cross a small plank bridge over a stream and follow the shady path alongside it. The path crosses and recrosses Login Brook several times before emerging on a broad grassy track. Continue ahead and emerge on the B4350.

10. Cross the road and turn right. Ignore a road on the left and a road to Capel y Ffin on the right. Turn left on a footpath signposted as St Mary's Road. On emerging from the enclosed path, cross the road. On your left is St Mary's Church.

11. After crossing the road, turn right and, in a few paces, go through a small gate. Follow a path below the motte and, on reaching a path junction, go left and cross another track. Descend steps and emerge on a path beside the River Wye. Turn right and in 500 metres, where the path passes under the B4351, take a path that zigzags up to the road.

12. Bear left to a junction. Turn right and pass The Granary Restaurant on your left. At the clock, bear left and take a right-hand cobbled way to another street. Bear right, then left through a small parking area and follow a wall below Hay Castle. Walk along Castle Lane and, at a junction, bear right to the car park and start of the walk.

10. Fan Frynych

Route: This straight forward moorland walk follows a level track before tackling a long, but gradual climb to Fan Frynych's 629 metre summit. There are impressive views of the nearby mountains.

Distance: 7 miles.

How to get there: Leave the A40 near Brecon to follow the A470 to Libanus. From their follow the road signs to the National Park Visitor Centre (the Mountain Centre).

Public Transport: Buses from Brecon and Merthyr Tydfil to Libanus, 1¼ miles from the start. On Sundays and Bank Holidays end of May to early September buses run from Brecon to the Mountain Centre.

Start: Brecon Beacons National Park Visitor Centre near Libanus.

Map: Outdoor Leisure 12.

The Brecon Beacons National Park Visitor Centre (Mountain Centre), situated at a height of over 1000 feet, makes a fine starting place for walks. Nearby are historical features. To the east is a Roman road and there are standing stones in the locality. The walk passes close to the

The Mountain Centre

edge of Traeth Mawr nature reserve, a swamp known for its interesting plants. Buzzard, peregrine and merlin may be seen on the route. In the Mountain Centre there is an informative display about the National Park.

The Tea Shop

From the terrace at the Mountain Centre Restaurant and Tea Room, you can enjoy panoramic views of the Brecon Beacons. Breakfast, morning coffee, lunch and afternoon teas are served and the varied menu includes hot soup, flans, salads, baps, and a wide selection of delicious cakes. Open 9.30am - 5.00pm (July and August closes at 6.00pm, November - February closes at 4.30pm). Open every day except Christmas Day. Tel: 01874 624979.

The Walk

1. From the Mountain Centre, walk out to the access lane and turn left. At its junction with a lane, where there is a cattle grid on the left, cross directly to a track. Ignore paths leading off and follow it to a road.

2. Cross directly over the road and continue along a shady lane. When the lane bends right to Forest Lodge, keep ahead on a rough track. Cross a stile at a gate and ignore a path on the left to Coed Ty-mawr. Follow the track through open land and ignore another track on the left. Pass above a forest and cross a stile at a gate to enter the Craig Cerrig-gleisiad nature reserve. Farther ahead, cross a stream and in approximately 100 metres, turn left on a grassy track.

3. Follow the track uphill towards trees. It bends to the left and eventually ends. Continue uphill on a path and pass a stone cairn before reaching the trig point on the summit of Fan Frynych (629m).

> Fan Frynych is the most northerly summit of the group of hills known as Fforest Fawr. The word fforest does not refer to trees, but is the medieval usage describing a tract of land used for hunting. The Norman lord Bernard de Neufmarche established Fforest Fawr and here he entertained his friends and guests. From Fan Frynych, in clear weather, there are fine views all around. To the

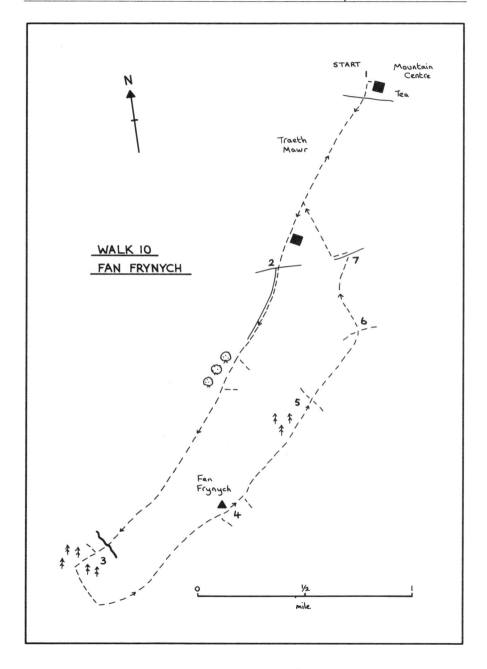

N

START

Mountain
Centre

Tea

Traeth
Mawr

WALK 10

FAN FRYNYCH

2

7

6

5

Fan
Frynych

4

3

0   ½   1

mile

east are the highest peaks in the National Park and all of South Wales, Pen y Fan and Corn Du. The lowest and most easterly of the Beacons is Cribyn. South are the crags of Cerrig-gleisiad and the plateau of Fan Fawr. Slightly west is the grassy bulk of Fan Llia and across the Llia valley is the summit of Fan Nedd.

4. From the trig point, maintain your direction on a grassy path. On reaching a wide track, turn left. The track soon starts to go downhill and, in about 400 metres, curves right to descend more steeply. Beyond a gate, it descends between fences and passes the remnants of coniferous trees.

5. On reaching a point where the track bends left, there is a stile on the right waymarked to the A470. Do not cross but walk ahead to another stile. Cross and follow the clear path ahead. On reaching a fence, and another path, bear left but, in a few paces, leave the main path to take a lesser path on the right. Follow the right-hand fence through trees for approximately 60 metres to a stile.

6. Keeping a fence nearby on the right, descend the field. When you reach the bottom right-hand corner, bear left to follow a path down to a stream and stepping stones. Take a clear path to the right. Cross the field to a stile near a gate.

7. Cross the road and turn left. In about 20 metres, climb the stile on the right. Veer slightly left across the field to a stile then slant right to the next one. Cross the next two fields diagonally left. Walk directly across a small field to the last stile. Bear right to retrace your steps along the track to the start of the walk at the Mountain Centre.

11. Llantwit Major

Route: Field paths and tracks lead to a cliff path on the Glamorgan Heritage Coast. The longer route passes through a nature reserve and visits St Donat's Church. There is much of historical interest on this walk as well as unspoilt coastal scenery.

Distance: 4¾ or 9 miles.

How to get there: Leave the A48 west of Glamorgan and take the B4270 to its junction with the B4265. Follow the signs to Llantwit Major.

Start: Car park at the Old Town Hall in Llantwit Major.

Map: Explorer 151.

Llantwit Major is a very ancient place. Iron Age promontory forts can be seen on the cliffs. Excavations in 1888 revealed evidence of Roman occupation when a mosaic floor and over forty human skeletons were found in a field near the town. The Roman villa was probably attacked by Irish pirates in the 4th century. The Old Town Hall was built in the 15th century after an earlier building was destroyed during the rebellion of Owain Glyndŵr. St Illtud, a native of Brittany, founded a monastery here in the 5th century, possibly on the site of the present church. It became a famous centre of learning and his pupils included Taliesin, David and Gildas the historian. St Illtud's Church is actually two churches built at different dates. In the west church are some early Christian stones and effigies. Wall paintings, memorial stones, a Norman font and a Jesse tree are some of the interesting features that can be seen in the church used for worship, the east church.

The Tea Shop

You will find Truffles Tea Room between the Old Town Hall and St Illtud's Church. In the cosy tearoom you can enjoy hot snacks such as home-made soup and filled jacket potatoes. Cream tea, Welsh tea and a delectable selection of cakes and pastries are also on offer. Open 10.00am - 5.00pm Monday to Friday, 9.30am - 5.00pm Saturday and 2.00pm - 6.00pm Sunday. Tel: 01446 792954.

The Walk

1. From the car park, walk out past the Old Town Hall. Turn left and ignore Burial Lane on the left. Pass Truffles Tea Room and, on reaching the church, bear left alongside the churchyard wall. When the lane bends right, go up a stepped path to Hill Head. Bear left and cross a stile on your right. Cross the field diagonally to pass the dovecote on your right.

> The limestone dovecote was built in the 13th century along with other monastic farm buildings owned by Tewkesbury Abbey. The great barn belonging to the grange stood to the north near the lane and gatehouse. In two fields farther north, excavations in the early 20th century revealed the remains of buildings including a cellar.

2. Walk downhill to the bottom right-hand corner and cross a stone stile. Emerge on a track known as Church Lane and bear left. In approximately 150 metres, ignore a stile on the left and follow the path around bends to arrive at a stone stile.

3. Cross the stile and follow the left-hand boundary of a long field to the next corner. Bear left to cross two stiles and descend a path through the valley known as Dimhole until you emerge on the cliff path. Bear right along the cliffs and go down steps to the stony beach at Tresilian Bay.

> Tresilian Bay derives its name from Prince Silian who may have had a court near here. At one time, the present house was an inn used by smugglers and pirates. It is said that long ago, a Breton pirate called Peter was buried up to his neck in a cave on the west side of the bay. Years previously, he had captured and held the smuggler Sir Henry Stradling to ransom. It was several months before the money was paid. Sir Henry wanted revenge and when the Breton eventually returned to the coast near St Donat's, Stradling recognised him and ordered his capture. Peter was left to drown on the incoming tide. On winter nights, when there is a full moon, his cries are carried on the wind. The bay also has romantic associations. An arch below the roof in the cave is called 'the bow of destiny' and it was used by lovers to find out when they would

Cliffs near Tresilian Bay

marry. The number of tries it took to throw a pebble that did not touch rock was the number of years they had to wait.

4. After walking across the beach, go up to the cliffs on the other side. In approximately 800 metres you have the option of shortening the walk by following a path on the right through the field to a lane, where you turn right and rejoin the longer walk at point 9. To continue on the longer walk, follow the coastal path through woodland and descend to St Donat's Bay.

> The Stradling family built the present St Donat's Castle in the 14th century. It is said they were pirates and smugglers. In the reign of Elizabeth I, Sir Thomas Stradling pretended to be a Protestant, but he was imprisoned for two years on the discovery of a cross in a fallen tree trunk. During the 18th century, the heir to the estate, Sir Thomas Stradling, went on a European tour accompanied by his friend Tyrrwhit. Stradling made a pact with his friend that if he died Tyrrwhit would inherit his estate. News came to St Donat's that Stradling had been killed at Montpelier whilst fighting a duel.

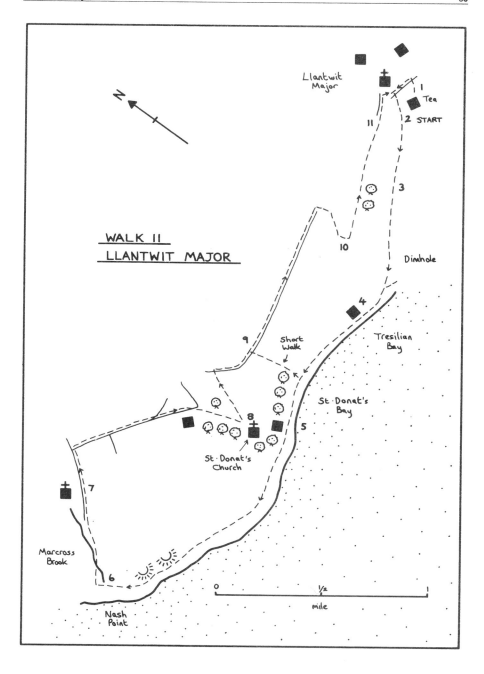

WALK II
LLANTWIT MAJOR

His body was brought back to the castle for burial. A nurse sitting by the coffin opened it to look at the dead body and she realised at once that it was not Sir Thomas; the heir had a finger missing but the corpse's hands were perfect. The real Sir Thomas never came back and eventually, after Tyrrwhit's death, the Tyrrwhit family inherited the castle whilst the Stradlings retained the baronetcy. The American newspaper magnate, William Randulph Hearst, bought the castle in the early 20th century. In 1962 it became an International sixth form college. It is now called Atlantic College.

5.   Go up steps on the other side of the bay and continue along the coast path. Pass two lighthouses on your right. Bear right to a small gate and follow the access lane to a parking area on the cliffs.

The Nash Point lighthouses were built after the Frolic wrecked on a nearby sandbank and forty people lost their lives. Only the west tower is in present use. On the west headland, Nash Point, is an Iron Age hill fort with four banks and three ditches. Melting glaciers during the Ice Age formed Cwm Marcroes. Woodpeckers may be present in the woodland.

6.   At a barrier on the left, leave the lane and follow a path downhill to the Marcroes brook. Cross a wide plank bridge and bear right to follow the stream on your right. Cross stepping stones over the brook and follow the right-hand path through the nature reserve. Emerge on a lane and turn left to Marcross church.

Dating from the 12th century, Marcross church has a Norman font and a 14th century tower. The sundial in the churchyard is mounted on the base of a medieval cross.

7.   Continue along the lane to the crossroad. Turn right and ignore an access lane on the right to Marcross Farm. In another 400 metres, turn right and follow a lane to where another meets it at Parc Farm. Pass the farm, go through a gate and walk ahead a short distance through the field to a small gate. Follow a path through woodland and, at a junction, take the left-hand path. It widens into a track and passes a ruin and another track on the right. On reaching a lane, turn right to St Donat's Church.

The first church at St Donat's was built in the early 12th century. When the castle was built, the church was enlarged and again 200 years later. Sir Thomas Stradling built the Lady Chapel in 1500 to contain tombs and memorials of the family. In the churchyard are two Calvary crosses. One is modern, but the cross on the south side is 15th century.

8. Leave the churchyard and walk uphill along the lane. Pass a parking area and follow a road past houses to some gates. Go through the small gate and turn right. After passing the grounds of St Donat's College, you will reach the point where the shorter route joins the lane.

9. Continue along the lane for just under a mile. Cross a stile on the right and follow the left-hand fence around two sides of a field. On reaching a pond, cross a stile and veer to the right through trees to another stile and emerge in a field. Walk along the left-hand boundary to a point where there is a stone stile on the left and directional arrows.

10. Climb the stile and walk through the field towards the left corner of some trees. Cross a stile and bear right to pass the wood. Continue ahead and, before reaching the end of the field, veer left to a stile in a wall. Walk ahead across the fields, crossing stiles, until you emerge on an enclosed path.

11. Turn left to follow the path to where it becomes a lane. Continue ahead and pass the gatehouse of the 13th century grange on the left. On reaching a junction, turn left and, at the next junction, bear right beside the churchyard to retrace your steps to Truffles Tea Room and the car park at the start of the walk.

12. Southgate

Route: A superb, varied walk taking in coast and woodland scenery. Some paths are rough underfoot for short sections and may be muddy after rain. Children must be closely supervised on the cliff paths.

Distance: 4½ miles.

How to get there: West of Swansea, leave the A4118 for the B4436. In ½ mile turn right for Southgate.

Public Transport: Buses from Swansea.

Start: National Trust car park on the cliffs at Southgate.

Map: Explorer 164.

Southgate is a popular starting place for coastal walkers and visitors to Threecliff Bay. On East Cliff is the large Minchin Hole cave, where excavations have revealed bones of animals now extinct, and Iron Age artefacts. The floor of the cave has a steep incline making it difficult to enter. Farther east, a steep path descends to Bacon Hole, another cave where animal bones were found. The name of the cave is derived from the dark red parallel stripes discovered in a side passage. Reminiscent of streaky bacon, they were once thought to be prehistoric cave paintings.

The Tea Shop

Three Cliffs Coffee Shop offers a welcome break to coast path walkers and visitors to nearby beaches. There are indoor and outdoor tables. The varied menu includes home-made soup, quiche, sandwiches, toasties and an excellent selection of home-made cakes. You may like to try the renowned Penclawdd cockles, which are gathered from the estuary on the north side of Gower. Open every day (except Christmas Day) from 10.30am.

The Walk

1. At the car park face the sea and bear left, to have the sea on your right. Follow a path around the cliffs. Emerge on a lane and continue along it to Hunts Farm.

2. Take a path on the right that descends across the top of a valley to reach a fence. Walk out to the cliffs near Pwlldu Head.

Cliffs at Pwlldu Head

Just west of Pwlldu Head is a small promontory hill fort, occupied in the late Iron Age up to the second century AD. There are two lines of ramparts cutting off the headland. Excavations revealed animal bones and pottery. South-east of Pwlldu Head is an area known as Graves End. An Admiralty vessel was wrecked near here in November 1760, bound for Plymouth with a hold of press-gang victims. Because of bad weather, the ship had turned about, and in poor light the crew thought Pwlldu headland was Mumbles Head. The vessel's bilges tore apart as she ground onto the rocks. Some men scrambled ashore, but those in the hold could not escape so easily. In the morning, local people found the ship breaking up and bodies being washed ashore. There were at least 68 dead and they were all buried in a common grave on the eastern slope of Pwlldu Head. The place they are buried is known as Graves End.

3. Follow the cliff top path. It passes through some gorse and bears left away from the cliff edge to descend a little before continuing on a fairly level path across a bracken-covered slope. At a path junction, turn left and walk uphill to a stile. Follow a fence on the left to a field.

4. Cross the middle of the field to a stile. Walk along the left boundary of a small field and pass through some trees and bushes to another stile. On reaching a track, do not turn right. Walk ahead and after passing through a gate, bear left. Almost immediately, turn right downhill on another track.

5. In approximately 100 metres, a few paces before the track reaches a house, bear right on a path. It descends through woodland. Just before the bottom of the hill, where the path makes a sharp right turn, go left on another path and pass a footbridge. (If you wish to visit the beach at Pwlldu Bay, cross the bridge over the stream and follow a track ahead uphill. In a few metres, take a footpath on the right.)

> Pwlldu means Black Pool and the name is derived from the pool behind the storm beach. The house nearest the pebble beach dates back to the 18th century when it was the Beaufort Inn. Much smuggling took place in the bay and the goods were taken through Bishopton valley to Great Highway and Little Highway Farms. The contraband was then hidden in cellars before being distributed throughout Gower. Limestone quarrying took place in the valley and there were several inns here. There is also an old lead mine. The Bishopton stream flows partly underground, but in wet weather is visible above ground most of the way through the valley.

6. With the stream on your right, follow the path inland through the woods of Bishopton Valley. In about 800 metres leave the stream to climb a stepped path. In about 100 metres it bears right and gradually returns to the valley floor. Bear left across rocks to have the stream on your right.

7. In approximately 100 metres, turn left away from the stream to follow another path. Cross a stile at a gate and bear slightly left on a wide stepped path. It becomes enclosed between fields. Go through a broad gate and continue ahead to pass in front of a house.

8. Bear left along the drive and emerge on a lane. Turn left along it. The lane veers right to emerge near the car park and coffee shop.

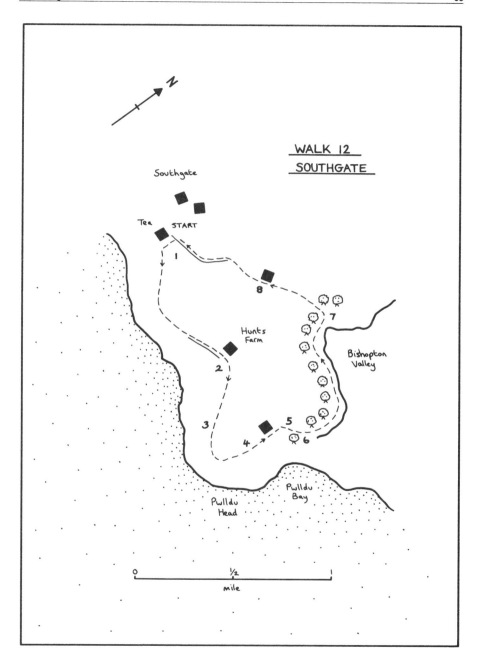

WALK 12
SOUTHGATE

13. Parkmill

Route: An interesting, varied walk taking in woodlands, a ridge walk, sand dunes, a ruined castle and prehistoric remains.

Distance: 5¾ miles.

How to get there: Parkmill is on the A4118, south-west of Swansea. Follow the signs for the Gower Heritage Centre.

Public Transport: Buses from Swansea and many villages on Gower.

Start: Car park at the Gower Heritage Centre. Parking is free for those visiting the centre, otherwise there is a charge.

Map: Explorer 164.

The Tea Shop

The Tearoom at the Gower Heritage Centre is in the mill complex, so allow plenty of time to look around. Attractions include a museum, farm animals, children's puppet theatre and play area. The old corn mill was built around 800 years ago by the Norman rulers of Gower, the de Braose family. The water wheel and machinery are still working and provide flour for the bread and cakes served in the tearoom. Traditional Welsh and cream teas are on offer as well as a variety of home baked cakes. Specialities include Teisen Lap, a cake made with sultanas and cream. Admission charges to the Heritage Centre include a Cream Tea Special – an inclusive charge for the centre and a Welsh cream tea. Open all year. Usual hours –10.00am - 5.00pm winter, 10.00am – 6.30pm summer (advisable to check). Tel. 01792 371206.

The Walk

1. On leaving the car park, face the mill complex entrance and turn left to cross the small footbridge over the stream. Turn right along the lane to enter Park Wood. In approximately 800 metres bear right with the lane but, almost immediately, leave it to go through a kissing gate. Walk through the long field, which is bordered by woodland. Pass a Neolithic burial chamber on your left.

The Parc le Breos Neolithic burial chamber is thought to be the best preserved in south-east Wales. After excavation in 1869 and 1960-1 it was partly restored. Made of local limestone, it is a long cairn with a passage and four small chambers. Bones of about twenty-four people, including three children, were found. Farther up this dry limestone valley, and above the right-hand side, the Cat Hole has revealed artefacts in use during the Palaeolithic period.

2. At the end of the field, the track reaches a junction. Turn left to follow another track through woodland. In about a kilometre, ignore minor tracks on the left and right. Follow the main track until you reach a turning area. Continue ahead on a path that bears left to a stile.

3. Turn right on a track to reach a fork. Take the left-hand track that goes ahead. In about 900 metres, pass a track on the right which leads to a farm. In another 100 metres, leave the track to go left on a grassy path uphill to the track running along the ridge of Cefn Bryn. As you ascend there are fine views over the north of Gower.

The red sandstone backbone of Cefn Bryn forms a fine ridge walk giving, in clear weather, spectacular views over Gower and across the Bristol Channel to Somerset and Devon. The main track, running the length of the hill, is known as Talbot's Road. It was named after the 19th century owner of Penrice Castle who used the track for hunting and riding. The summit of Cefn Bryn (passed on the walk) is the second highest point in Gower. At the eastern end of the hill, look for The Gower Way Stone, which was unveiled in 1998 by HRH the Prince of Wales.

4. Turn left along the track. At first it goes uphill and views open up of Oxwich Bay. Descend to a junction and continue ahead to join a lane. Follow it past a car park. Go through a kissing gate at a cattle grid and follow the lane to the A4118 on the edge of Penmaen.

5. Cross the road directly and follow the lane ahead. On reaching a junction, turn right and walk downhill. Follow the lane as it bends left. In a few metres, where the lane becomes a track and

Threecliff Bay

veers to the left, continue ahead on a path to have fine views of Threecliff Bay.

Three pointed cliffs give the name to the beautiful spot known as Threecliff Bay. It is dangerous to bathe in the sea here. In 1917 barrels of French wine were washed ashore in the bay and it is said that within the space of an hour two hundred people were on the beach with all manner of receptacles to carry it home. (Few carried it that far!).

6. The path emerges at the stream known as Pennard Pill. Cross the stream by stepping stones and bear left to follow a path below sandhills and Pennard Castle. (If the stepping stones should be impassable, retreat along the lane and bear right at the junction. Go through a farmyard and continue on an enclosed track. It eventually enters woodland and descends to the main road. Bear right and cross to a lane. In 100 metres retrace your steps over the footbridge to the mill complex.)

The impressive ruins of Pennard castle stand in a beautiful position above the valley of the Pennard Pill. If you climb the sand dunes to inspect them you will find the stronghold is a mere shell. A castle

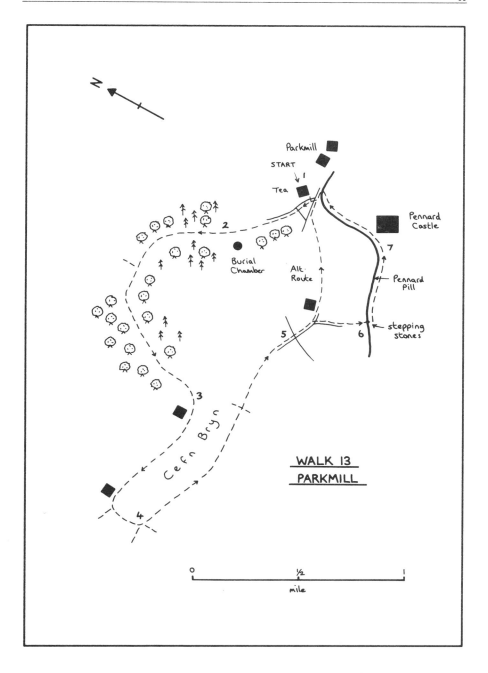

WALK 13
PARKMILL

with a ditch and bank was built here in the 12th century but only the footings of this early fortress remain. A century or two later, the castle was rebuilt in local limestone and sandstone by the de Braose family, the Norman rulers of Gower. The castle had a curtain wall around a courtyard and a twin-towered gatehouse. A small settlement grew close to the castle, but severe gales in the following centuries caused the castle, church and village to be gradually overwhelmed by sand and the whole area was abandoned. A legend tells another version of the abandonment. Whilst celebrating his marriage feast, a chieftain of Pennard Castle was disturbed by fairy music and, inflamed by wine and rage, with his troops, he tried to kill the fairy elves. Being bodiless, the elves could not be slain by the repeated stabbings. Eventually, a voice spoke to the chief telling him that his war against them had destroyed him. He had spoilt their innocent sport and for this his township and castle would be no more. As the elf raised his wand, whirlwinds of sand rushed to overwhelm the castle and houses. It was said the sand had come from Ireland.

7. After walking below Pennard Castle and passing through a sandy area, continue on the main path and ignore narrow paths leading off it. The path bears right to cross a footbridge over the stream. On reaching the main road, bear left. In a few metres, cross the road to follow a lane to the mill and start of the walk.

14. Oxwich

Route: A varied walk following lanes, a coastal path above low cliffs and through woodland.

Distance: 5 miles.

How to get there: Oxwich is on the south coast of Gower, off the A4118 and west of Swansea.

Public Transport: Buses from Swansea.

Start: Oxwich car park, the crossroads and beach.

Map: Explorer 164.

Oxwich is a small, attractive seaside village situated at the western end of a magnificent sweep of sands. Much of the bordering land is a nature reserve. In the 19th century, quarrying took place above the beach and the limestone was shipped to Devon to be converted to lime. John Wesley stayed in the village on his missionary tour of the peninsula.

The coast near Oxwich Point

The Tea Shop

The terraced garden of the Oxwich Hotel is a very popular stop for walkers and visitors to the beautiful sandy Oxwich Bay. Refreshments may also be taken in the Garden Room. The varied menu includes main dishes, pasta, salads, cream teas and Welsh cakes. Open 9.00am - 10.00pm daily. Tel: 01792 390329.

The Walk

1.   From the car park walk back to the main road and turn left. On reaching the crossroads, cross directly and take the lane uphill, signposted to Oxwich Castle. Ignore two footpaths into woodland. Continue uphill until you reach a track on the left signposted to Oxwich Castle. Follow it to a fork. Take the left fork if you wish to visit the castle.

> The romantic ruins of Oxwich Castle stand on the site of an earlier Norman castle. Sir Rice Mansel, who inherited the Oxwich and Penrice estates, rebuilt the castle in the early 16th century. It was really a fortified Tudor manor house. After Sir Rice moved to Margam, his eldest son stayed and built the huge east block. However, by the early 17th century, it was occupied by tenant farmers. The Mansel crest can still be seen above the gateway. In 1557, the Mansels and villagers looted a French ship that wrecked in Oxwich Bay. Sir George Herbert of Swansea marched to Oxwich to claim the spoils. In the affray that followed under the castle gateway, Edward Mansel's aunt, Anne Mansel, was struck on the head by a stone. She later died. Sir George was fined and ordered to return the loot.

2.   The walk continues along the right-hand track. In approximately 50 metres, cross a stile on the right into a field. Walk across to the far corner where two hedges meet. Cross a stone stile on the left and follow the lane to Oxwich Green.

3.   Continue along the lane and ignore a footpath on the left. After passing houses, the lane narrows and there are fine views on the left across fields to the sea. Ignore a bridleway on the right and

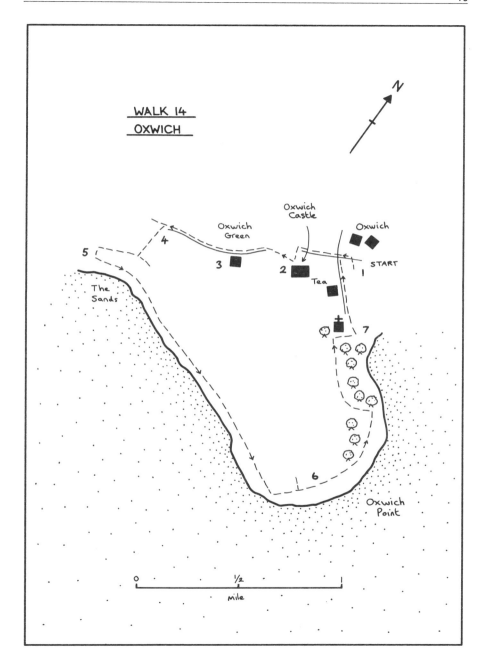

follow the lane downhill. Pass a farm on the right and reach a fork.

4. Turn left, downhill. Go through a gap beside a gate. In another 50 metres, ignore a kissing gate on the left and bear right to another kissing gate. Follow a clear path between bushes. It bears to the right and passes below crags. At a gate ahead, climb a stile on the left. Follow an enclosed path and emerge on the coastal footpath.

5. Cross a stile on the left. Follow the coast path above a sandy cove. Cross more stiles. At one point the path has eroded and it is necessary to divert into a field. Farther on, the walk passes under crags then rises to a stile near a gate. Walk on towards Oxwich Point. At a path junction, turn right.

6. Cross a stile to enter Oxwich National Nature Reserve. Follow the path through woodland. In places it is stepped. The path goes alongside the wood boundary then goes downhill to meet a flight of steps. Bear right to descend them. On reaching the bottom, turn left above the bay. Pass St Illtyd's Church on the left.

> The little church of St Illtyd is charmingly situated amongst trees beside the sea. Foundations date from the 6th century. The small chancel may have been a Celtic cell. According to local tradition, the font was brought to Oxwich by St Illtyd himself. Inside the church are recumbent effigies of a knight and his lady. A ghost of a white horse is said to haunt the churchyard. The old rectory, which was sited nearer the sea, was destroyed by a violent storm in 1805.

7. Continue along a broad track. Pass Oxwich Bay Hotel on the left. Veer right to return to the start of the walk and the car park.

15. Port Eynon

Route: This superb, coastal walk boasts spectacular cliff scenery and much historical interest. The longer walk returns through fields.

Distance: 2¾ or 6½ miles

How to get there: From Swansea take the A4118 to Port Eynon.

Public Transport: Buses from Swansea.

Start: Car park near the beach at Port Eynon.

Map: Explorer 164.

The name Port Eynon is thought to be derived from Eynon, a Welsh prince who lived in the 11th century. It is said he built a castle that disappeared long ago. Nowadays, Port Eynon is a quiet seaside village, very popular with families. Until the early 20th century, villagers earned their living from oyster dredging and quarrying. In the mid 19th century, thirty to forty oyster skiffs operated out of Port Eynon to dredge the Bantum oyster bed, which lies off the sandbank called Helwick Sands. Overdredging led to a decline and the industry ended here about 1879. The oyster season was October to February and quarrying took place during the summer months. Limestone was shipped to Bideford and Barnstaple in Devon. Another occupation was smuggling and, at one time, eight excisemen were stationed in the village. The wrecking of the steamship Agnes Jack at Port Eynon Point, with the loss of twenty lives, led to a lifeboat station being established at Port Eynon in 1884. It is now a youth hostel. A Miss Maria Jones of Lancaster donated the money and she requested the lifeboat to be called *A Daughter's Offering*. She was followed by Janet in 1906, who tragically lost three crew in 1916, when going to the assistance of *SS Dunvegan* in Oxwich Bay. A memorial to the men may be seen in St Cattwg's churchyard. After this rescue attempt, the lifeboat was withdrawn.

The Tea Shop

The Smugglers Haunt is a licensed restaurant with a tea room and outdoor tables, near the beach at Port Eynon. Afternoon teas are served and the Smugglers Haunt is usually open all day from the beginning of March to the end of November. Tel: 01792 391257.

The Walk

1. Leave the car park by the car entrance and cross the track to another track directly opposite. In about 200 metres, go through a kissing gate and cross a camp site to another stile. Do not go through the gate ahead – unless you wish to visit the Salt House. (Return to this point afterwards.)

   The forlorn ruins to be seen at Salt House are the remains of two 18th century cottages, salt pans and a stone quay. Below the ruins are the cellars of the old Salt House mansion, which was built in the 16th century by David Lucas of Stout Hall (near Knelston) for his son John Lucas. Before getting married, John Lucas had spent a roving life. He could not settle, and with other lawless young men he smuggled, and wrecked ships. Being a Robin Hood type of character, he shared his spoils with poor villagers. Seven generations later, a John Lucas living at Salt House discovered a means of producing red and black paint from iron-stained shales. In 1703 a great storm flooded the Salt House mansion and after the family escaped, it was never occupied again. According to local legend, the last smuggled cargo of silk and brandy still lies buried in the cellars.

2. Follow the enclosed path away from the sea. On reaching a path junction, turn left. In about 100 metres, bear right on a path that climbs through quarry debris and gorse. Follow a level stretch of path to a path junction on the cliff top. From near this point, an unofficial path descends to a lower path from where it is possible, with care, to scramble over rock to view the Culver Hole.

   Although rather awkward to reach, and not recommended for young children, a visit to Culver Hole should not be missed. This intriguing walled in cave has a 60 foot wall of masonry with openings or 'windows'. The reason for building it is a mystery. Although it was once used as a dovecote, the cave may also have been a smugglers' retreat. The first John Lucas of Salt House is said to have repaired and rebuilt 'Kulverd Hall' for use as a stronghold and store for arms. It was reached by means of an underground passage. Another theory suggests Culver Hole may have been a stronghold and dovecote for Port Eynon Castle. It can only be reached at low tide.

3. On the cliff top, bear right. In about 150 metres, descend a rough path to Overton Mere. Turn right to cross a stile and, on reaching a path junction, ignore a right-hand path and continue around the bay. In about 400 metres, leave the main path to go left on a path leading to a stile. Follow a path around Overton Cliff to the next stile.

Culver Hole

Above the valley is a natural limestone cave with a low passage that extends into the hillside for about 45 feet. Known as the Long Hole cave, it was excavated in 1861 and again in 1969. Finds of flint tools and animal bones indicate occupation by man in 30,000BC. The sea level at that time was lower than it is now and there would have been a plain below the cliffs.

4. Bear right on a path between outcrops and ascend the valley below Longhole Cliff. Reach a junction with a bridleway. (If following the short walk, turn right and follow the bridleway to a lane. Continue past Overton Green. Skip all directions before Point 9.)

5. If following the longer walk, turn left and, in approximately 60 metres, cross a stile at a gate. Follow the right-hand fence over a number of stiles. Pass above Common Cliff and its spectacular cliff scenery. About 1½ miles from Longhole, the path drops into Foxhole Slade.

The famous Paviland Cave can be reached by scrambling over rocks at the bottom of Foxhole Slade. Excavations in 1823 by William Buckland revealed a skeleton. Alongside it were votive offerings of ivory rings and perforated shells. All were stained by red ochre and the skeleton became known as the 'Red Lady of Paviland'. The skeleton was, in fact, a male about 25 years old and it is thought the burial took place in the Upper Palaeolithic era, about 26,000 years ago. Many flint tools, and animal bones, including those of mammoth, wolf, woolly rhino and hyena, were also found.

6. At this point, the walk leaves the coast. Bear right to cross a stile and follow a left-hand hedge. Cross two more stiles and continue ahead over a small footbridge and stile. In about 250 metres, ignore a stile on the left. Walk ahead to reach a footbridge. Do not cross but bear right to have a ditch on your left. On reaching a farm access lane, turn right.

7. When the farm lane turns right, go left between barns and continue on a track. It bears right to enter a field. Follow the track to a gate. Do not go through it but bear left beside a hedge to reach a stile. Slant slightly right across the next field and follow a right-hand hedge to a corner stile. Continue beside right-hand hedges, crossing stiles. Bear left to pass behind the buildings of Hills farm, which is on your left.

8. Cross a stile and walk ahead a few metres. Slant to the right across the field towards a corner fence, and walk towards the sea. Follow the right-hand fence to a stile and bear left to reach a track. Turn right and follow it to a lane. Pass a farm on the left and at Overton Green, turn left.

9. After passing a farm, cross a stile on the right. Walk ahead to cross stiles and follow the path as it veers left. After crossing another stile, enter a caravan site and walk downhill. Bear left through the site to the road in Port Eynon. Turn right to the car park and Smugglers Haunt Restaurant.

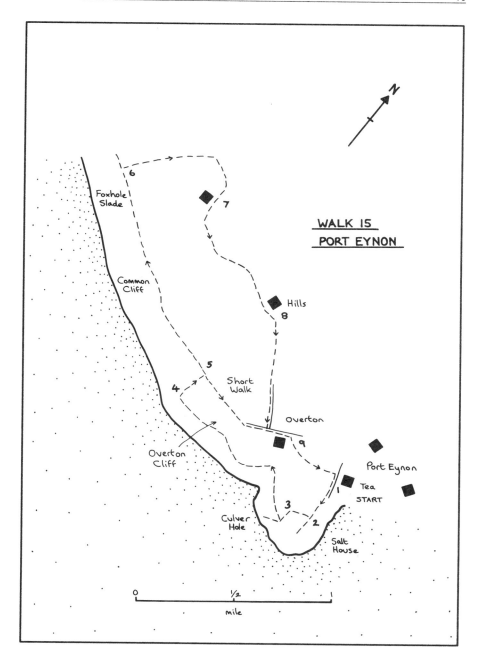

N

WALK 15
PORT EYNON

Foxhole
Slade

Common
Cliff

6

7

Hills
8

5

Short
Walk

4

Overton
Cliff

Overton

9

Port Eynon

Tea
START

1

3

2

Culver
Hole

Salt
House

0   ½   1
mile

16. Rhossili

Route: A superb walk with outstanding views of Worms Head. After climbing to the top of Rhossili Down, the longer route returns to the start by following a section of cliff path.

Distance: 4 or 7½ miles.

How to get there: From Swansea take the A4118. Leave it at Scurlage to take the B4247 to Rhossili.

Public Transport: Buses from Swansea.

Start: Car park at the end of the road in Rhossili.

Map: Explorer 164.

Perched on top of 200 foot cliffs, Rhossili is the most westerly village in Gower. Much of the land around the village belongs to the National Trust and there is a Visitor Centre and shop in the old coastguard cottages. The earliest settlement here was an Iron Age promontory fort, sited about 400 metres west of the car park. In 1979, excavations on the terrace at the foot of Rhossili Down discovered the remains of Celtic houses and part of a church. Encroaching sand may have caused the abandonment of the settlement. The present church has a Norman doorway and saddleback tower. Inside there is a memorial tablet to Petty Officer Edgar Evans who died in Captain Scott's expedition to the South Pole. At the south end of Rhossili Bay, the wooden ribs of a ship can be seen sticking out of the sand. These are the remains of the *Helvetia*, which grounded after being blown around Worms Head during a south-easterly gale in November 1887. All the crew escaped and her 500 ton cargo of timber was salvaged. However, the wrecking of the oak barque led to a tragedy. A vessel that loaded some of the timber left an anchor behind. The boat sent to recover it capsized and five men drowned.

The Tea Shop

Thomas's Tea Room is in a fine position overlooking Rhossili Bay. The varied menu includes salads, pies, home-made cakes and cream teas. Refreshments can be taken outside in the tea garden. Open 9.30am - 6.00pm (4.30pm early and late in the season) from February to the end of October. Arrangements can be made for the tea room to open in the winter. Tel: 01792 390519.

The cliffs and bay below Rhossili

The Walk

1. From the car park, walk back along the road. Pass the church and immediately turn left on a track. Emerge on Rhossili Down. Do not go uphill, but walk ahead to have a wall on the left. Look back for fine views of Rhossili village and Worms Head. In about 900 metres, you will pass the Old Rectory.

> Because the vicar of Rhossili church also served Llangennith, the Old Rectory was built halfway along the Downs. Built in 1850, the present house has been renovated and is now owned by the National Trust.

2. Continue ahead on a clear path to have a wall nearby on the left. Pass a caravan site on the left. On reaching the end of the site (the entrance) there is a gate giving access to the lane. Do not go through it, but turn right on a steep, clear path to ascend Rhossili Down.

> At 632 feet, the Beacon on top of Rhossili Down is the highest point on Gower. North of the summit, on the gentle east slopes, are the remains of two Neolithic tombs called Sweyn's Howes. The

name is derived from Sweyn, the Viking, and legendary founder of Swansea. The tombs are traditionally the grave of Sweyn. Near the path across the Down and about 100 metres before the summit, is a Bronze Age ring cairn consisting of stones and a level platform.

3.   After passing rocky outcrops, take a narrower path on the left. It soon bears right and continues along the ridge of Rhossili Down. Pass the remains of a wartime radar station and follow a broad track uphill to the summit.

4.   Continue along the ridge. The path soon descends and in about 300 metres you will see a wall and fence to the left of the path. (If following the shorter walk, continue downhill to join your outward route at the gate giving access to Rhossili Down. Retrace your steps to the start and tea room.) The longer route turns left, at this point, to have the wall and fence on the right. Pass behind a house and, in about 120 metres, reach a path junction. (This is about 30 metres before a reservoir.) Bear right and descend to a lane.

5.   Turn right along the lane and go through a kissing gate at a cattle grid. The lane leads to the B4247 in Middleton. Cross the road with care and turn left. In about 70 metres the pavement ends. Continue about another 30 metres, then turn right on a track. It soon narrows into a path between hedges. Go through a small gate and emerge on the National Trust land of Mewslade.

The impressive headland to the south-east (on your left across the valley) is Thurba Head. On this promontory is an Iron Age hill fort, one of five between Port Eynon Point and Worms Head. The sands of Mewslade Bay are covered for about three hours at high water. Its cliffs are popular with climbers.

6.   Walk ahead and, in 30 metres, you will reach a fork. Take the right-hand path and ignore a path descending into the valley. Follow the path nearest the fence or wall to have fine views of Mewslade and Thurba Cliff. On reaching the cliff-top, pass above Mewslade Bay and continue beside the wall. As you climb higher there are fine views of the beach and cliffs.

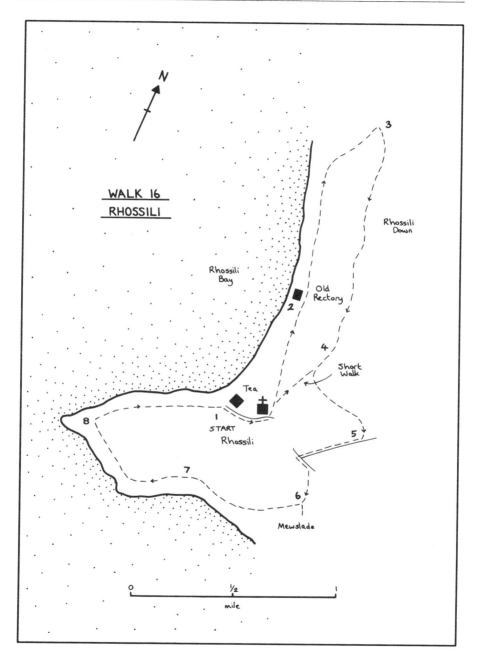

N

WALK 16
RHOSSILI

Rhossili Down

Rhossili
Bay

Old
Rectory

2

3

4

Short
Walk

Tea

1
START
Rhossili

8

7

5

6

Mewslade

0   ½   1
mile

7. The path climbs and veers away from the wall before descending a little above Fall Bay to reach a junction of paths. Keep ahead on the undulating path. Bear right with the wall to have views of Worms Head. Stay by the wall when it bends right. At the next corner, take the path ahead to the Old Coastguard Lookout Visitor Centre. It is the starting point for visiting Worms Head.

    An island at high water, Worms Head is the most westerly point of Gower. The name comes from Wurm or Orm, meaning dragon or sea serpent. The causeway is only open for about 2½ hours either side of low water. It is advisable to leave Worm for the mainland not later than 3½ hours before high water. Fatalities have occurred to those trying to swim back. The crossing is not recommended for young children or the less agile. The Worm is a mile long and the whole headland covers about 37 acres. The inner head is completely flat. After the middle head there is a natural rock bridge called Devil's Bridge. The outer head has a blow hole in which a small fissure, connected to a sea cave, produces strange roaring sounds that can be heard in Rhossili. The bones of mammoth and other extinct animals have been found in another cave. Guillemots and razorbills breed on the cliffs.

8. From the lookout, turn right towards Rhossili Down to have superb views of Rhossili Bay. On reaching a wall, continue on a wide track. After passing the National Trust Visitor Centre on the right, you will reach the car park and, a little farther on, Thomas's Tea Room.

17. Llangennith

Route: This delightful walk takes in lanes, cliffs, fields and dune paths as well as a beautiful sandy beach. A small island may be visited at high tide.

Distance: 6 or 6¼ miles.

How to get there: Llangennith is located on the west side of the Gower peninsula. From Swansea take the A4118 to Killay then the B4271 to Llanrhidian. Continue on minor roads to Llangennith.

Public Transport: Buses from Swansea.

Start: Village green near the church in Llangennith.

Map: Explorer 164.

Llangennith is known as 'Llangenny' by local people. The church, which is the largest in Gower, was founded by St Cenydd. According to legend, he was the offspring of an incestuous relationship between a Celtic prince and the prince's own daughter. Because of this sin, Cenydd was born a cripple and his parents placed him in a wicker basket that they abandoned on the River Lliw, which flows into the River Loughor. The cradle drifted ashore onto Worms Head where seagulls cared for him. According to other versions of the story, the cradle came to rest on Burry Holms. When he reached manhood he went to college at Llantwit Major and studied religion. He returned to Llangennith and founded a church and college. Vikings destroyed the church by fire in AD986. A new church was built by the Normans as part of the Abbey of St Taurin at Evreux in Normandy. In exchange for protection from raiders, the monks gave away some of their land. The Norman De la Mare family became important landowners in the area and an effigy of one of their knights may be seen inside the church. Another interesting relic is St Cenydd's burial stone. The church tower has a saddleback roof. The remains of the village well are on the green opposite the lych gate.

The Tea Shop

From Llangennith Post Office Tea Room there is a lovely view towards the sea. Refreshments may also be taken at tables on the terrace. Breakfasts, cream teas and a variety of sandwiches and cakes are on offer. Usual hours 9.00am - 5.30pm. Closes early at weekends out of season. Tel: 01792 386201.

The Walk

1. From the village green, take the road towards the beach. Pass the post office and, on reaching a road junction, take the first lane on the right. From this undulating lane views stretch to the burrows, Worms Head and Rhossili Down.

2. At the lane end, continue on a track. Go through a gate and walk downhill towards Broughton Farm and a caravan site. When the track bends to the right, climb over a stile on the left. Cross a small field to another stile. Continue beside a right-hand fence, crossing several stiles. Emerge on a track near Broughton Farm and turn left.

3. Walk towards the caravan site. Follow a tarmac track and bear right at a post with a yellow arrow. In a few metres, when the track ends, follow a footpath signposted to Blue Pool. A clear path passes above cliffs and through the burrows for about 900 metres before arriving at Blue Pool Corner.

Blue Pool Corner is sometimes known as Blue Pool Bay. The pool is a natural circular rock pool, about 15 feet across. Gold doubloons and moidores were discovered nearby in 1770 by a couple fishing from nearby rocks. A ship carrying gold had probably wrecked in the bay sometime earlier. It is unlikely that all the lost coins have been found. West of the bay is an arch known as Three Chimneys and, beyond it, a cave called Culver Hole (not to be confused with the Culver Hole at Port Eynon). A narrow slit leads to a large chamber where the bones of 30-40 people were found, along with Bronze Age urns. The cave is only accessible at low water.

4. Continue along the main path. It descends to emerge on the beach near the island of Burry Holms.

Burry Holms is a small limestone island at the northern tip of Rhossili Bay. It is only accessible at low tide. An Iron Age earthwork bisects the island and there are ruins of a medieval monastic settlement on the sheltered eastern side. Excavations carried out 1965-7 revealed stone foundations of a small 12th century church, hall and other buildings on the site of an earlier settlement. In

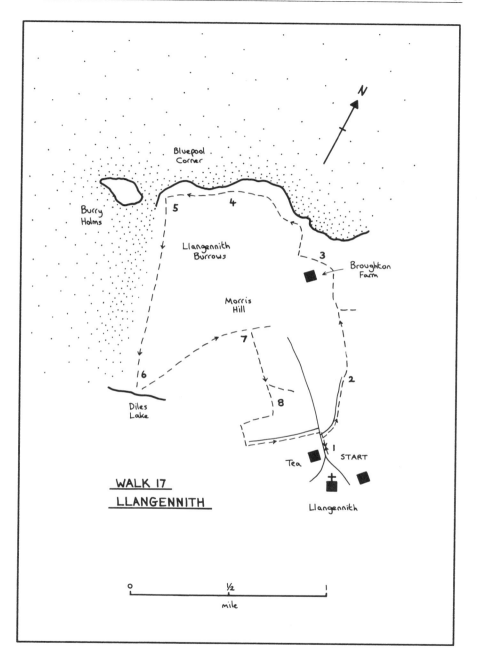

WALK 17
LLANGENNITH

Burry Holms

. November 1840, a small paddle steamer called the City Of Bristol
wrecked south of Burry Holms on her way to Waterford. On board
were 17 crew, 7 passengers, 18 cattle and 100 pigs. After enduring
much pounding, the vessel broke in two during the night. Only two
people and a few pigs and cattle survived.

5. With the sea on your right, walk south along the beach. Worms
    Head is in view ahead and, on your left, the hill called Rhossili
    Down. After a mile, you will reach a stream called Diles Lake.

    The Cleveland, a World War II Destroyer, was stranded on the beach
    near Diles Lake for several months during the summer of 1957.
    Whilst being towed from Cardiff to Llanelli to be scrapped, she broke
    loose and drifted ashore to Diles Lake where she became stuck.
    After several attempts to refloat her failed, she was broken up on
    the beach. In the 17th century, a vessel, which became known as The
    Dollar Ship, wrecked south of Diles Lake. A Mr Mansel is said to
    have taken most of her silver, and then vanished. His ghost haunts
    the bay in a black coach pulled by four grey horses. In the early 19th
    century, the hulk was exposed and piles of Spanish coins dated

1625 and 1639 were recovered. Many local people benefited from the spoils.

6. Turn left to have the stream on your right, and follow it to a stile near a gate. Continue on a wide, clear path through dunes and past reedbeds. Stay on the main path and cross a stile near a gate. With Morris Hill above on your left, follow a fence uphill. After descending for about 100 metres, look for a stile a few metres to the right. (An alternative, easier way back by road, is to continue on the main path to another stile. Go ahead and, when you meet the access lane to Broughton Farm Caravan Park, turn right to the lane junction met earlier.)

7. After crossing the stile, follow the left boundary of fields. Cross two stiles and another near gates. Continue along the left side of a field and ignore a field gate on the left. Walk beside a hedge to another stile and cross a narrow field to the next stile. (In dry weather, a shorter route may be taken here, by bearing left to a stile and following the left side of the field to a corner. Continue on a narrow, rather brambly and possibly muddy path. Emerge on a lane and turn right to the lane junction.)

8. The longer route ignores the stile on the left and continues along the left side of the field to another stile. Walk ahead and before reaching the field corner, turn right to follow a hedge on the left. Cross two stiles and, at the end of the last field, bear left through a gap. Veer right to go through two gates and follow an embankment. Go left to cross a bridge over a stream. Climb a stile and cross the field to a stile and lane. Turn left to the crossroads and bear right to the tea room and start of the walk.

18. Amroth

Route: This is a fairly easy walk along woodland tracks, paths and lanes. The walk starts with a long, but gentle, climb to the famous Colby Woodland Gardens.

Distance: 3¾ miles.

How to get there: Amroth is located on the coast north-east of Tenby. Leave the A477 near Kilgetty for a minor road to Amroth.

Public Transport: Buses from Tenby and Carmarthen.

Start: Amroth car park.

Map: Outdoor Leisure 36.

Amroth is an attractive seaside village with a bank of shingle separating the road from the sand. Stone Age flints have been found on the beach. At exceptionally low tides, the tree stumps of a forest submerged about 5000BC are visible at the water's edge. In the 19th century, there was a row of cottages on the seaward side of the road, but they have been gradually washed away by the sea, during winter storms. The area was known for its high quality coal which, being smokeless and odourless, was sought for the drying of malt and hops. The present Amroth Castle is a castellated house that was built about the beginning of the 19th century. Earlier castles named Earweare stood on the site or nearby. It is said that, in medieval times, Cadwgan ap Bleddyn held a banquet here and Gerald of Windsor and his beautiful wife Nest were among the guests. Some time later, Cadwgan's son Owain abducted Nest and hid her at World's End near Llangollen.

The Tea Shop

On this walk you can take a break for refreshments en route or/and in Amroth.

The Bothy Tea Room at the National Trust property Colby Woodland Garden has some of its seating in the former stables. The menu includes hot soup, fresh and toasted sandwiches and home-made scones. Local Welsh cheeses are on offer. Open 11.00am - 5.00pm. April until the end of October. Tel: 01834 811885.

The Pirate Restaurant is located on the sea front in Amroth, opposite the beach. The extensive menu includes grills, omelettes, vege-

Amroth beach

tarian meals, pastas, breakfasts, sandwiches, cream teas and Welsh cake. There is outdoor seating. Open 9.00am - 8.30pm from Easter to the end of October. Tel: 01834 812757.

The Walk

1. From the car park, walk towards the sea front and turn left. Ignore the lane on the left to Amroth church. Continue beside the sea and in approximately 350 metres, turn left on a bridleway.

2. In a few metres the track bears left between houses and shortly veers right. Follow the broad track through a mixed wood. Pass a house on the left and walk uphill. Ignore a track on the right. In another 200 metres, where a track joins from a gate on the right, turn left and follow the main track to a surfaced lane.

3. Walk ahead and ignore a track on the right to Trelessy Farm. Turn left on a track to Eastlake Farm. Pass a house and, in about 50 metres before reaching more buildings, go through a gap in

the fence on the left. Cross a track to pass through a similar gap. Bear right to follow a fence on the right and pass farm buildings. Walk ahead and cross a stile near a gate.

4. Follow a clear path between hedges and trees. It shortly goes downhill to cross a slab over a stream. In approximately 20 metres, take a path on the right. As you walk uphill, views extend towards the sea. Cross a stile and walk ahead to have trees on your left. The path descends to a stile and lane. Turn right and pass Amroth church on your left.

> The parish church of Amroth is dedicated to St Elidyr who lived in the 6th century. At one time the church was in the hands of the Knights Hospitallers of St John of Jerusalem. The present building dates from the 13th century. The Chantry Chapel was added by John Elliott of Amroth Castle and additional enlargement and rebuilding took place in the 19th century. The church contains some interesting monuments and, in the churchyard, there are the steps of a 9th century preaching cross.

5. From the church gates continue uphill. Pass the Old School on your left. In 100 metres turn left to walk along another lane. Follow the lane when it bends left to Colby Gardens.

> Known for its superb collection of rhododendrons and azaleas, Colby Woodland Gardens is one of the loveliest of the National Trust's properties. It is worth visiting at any time during the season for its tranquillity, views and woodland walks. It is difficult to imagine that, in the 18th and early 19th centuries, the valley was mined for anthracite and iron ore. One of the industrialists was John Colby who built Colby Lodge around 1803. About 100 years ago, Major Kay bought the Colby Estate and planted the Woodland Garden, partly with rhododendrons that his brother had collected in the Himalayas. Later generations of the Kay family, and Mr Peter Chance, who owned part of the estate for a time, continued to make improvements. The estate was given to the National Trust in the early 1980s. Although not maintained by the NT, the charming walled garden, with its gazebo, is usually open to the public visiting Colby Woodland Gardens. Open from early April to the end of

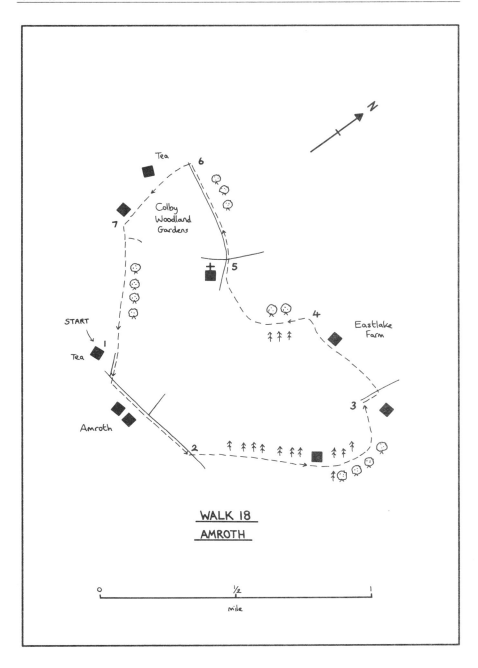

Tea

6

Colby
Woodland
Gardens

7

5

4

Eastlake
Farm

START

Tea

1

3

Amroth

2

WALK 18

AMROTH

0   ½   1

mile

October 10.00am - 5.00pm. (Walled garden hours a little shorter.)
- Admission charge (free to NT members).

6. If not visiting the gardens, continue along the lane and pass a high wall on the left. Turn left on a surfaced track signposted 'To the Coast Path'. It passes the walled garden on the left and the tea room on your right. Continue ahead along the main track. After going downhill, it reaches a three-way footpath signpost.

7. Turn left and, at another post, continue ahead. When the track emerges on a private road, walk ahead to join a lane. Turn right and descend towards the sea. The car park is on your right. To visit the Pirate Restaurant, walk out to the sea front and turn right.

19. Tenby

Route: A coastal walk from the beautiful seaside resort of Tenby to the small cove at Waterwynch Bay. There is the option of a diversion to Monkstone Beach.

Distance: 4½ or 7½ miles.

How to get there: Leave the A477 south of Kilgetty and follow the A478 to Tenby.

Public Transport: Trains from Swansea and Pembroke. Buses from Haverfordwest, Carmarthen, Narbeth and Amroth.

Start: South Beach car park, Tenby.

Map: Outdoor Leisure 36.

The Welsh name for the picturesque seaside resort of Tenby is Dinbych-y-pysgod, 'little fort of the fishes'. Little is known of the town's early history, except that it was a Welsh stronghold in the 9th century. When the Normans arrived, they built a castle on the headland between the North and South Sands. The town walls, built in the 13th century, were strengthened in the 1450s and again during the time of the Armada.

Tenby harbour and North Beach

Tenby became a busy port, but trade declined and by the early 19th century, the town had become a fashionable resort. It became a Georgian watering place, and the coming of the railway in Victorian times brought more tourists. There is much of interest to see in Tenby. St Mary's Church dates from the 13th century and has some interesting effigies, tombs and wall tablets. On Castle Hill there is a museum. The Tudor Merchant's House, owned by the National Trust, is also worth a visit. From Easter to October, there are boat trips to Caldy Island. At high tide, they leave from the harbour and at low water from Castle Beach, below the headland. Caldy is owned by a monastic order and boats do not cross to the island on Sundays.

The Tea Shop

The Upper Crust Tea Room in the High Street offers hot meals, salads and a wide selection of snacks. Cream tea, Welsh tea and home-made apple pie are generally available. Usual hours 10.00am to 5.00pm. Tel: 01834 842502.

The Walk

1. From the car park, walk towards the sea and shortly bear left to follow a zigzag path uphill. At a junction, bear right to the Esplanade. Walk along with the sea on your right and follow the road as it turns left. Bear right through an arch and pass the Imperial Hotel. Veer right to continue above the beach and follow the streets nearest the sea

2. On reaching the harbour, if you wish to walk around Castle Hill, follow a path past the museum and around the headland. After passing the lifeboat station, it returns to the harbour. Turn right, downhill to pass St Julien's Church and Tenby Sailing Club. Continue above North Beach. Before reaching an ice cream kiosk, go left up steps and emerge on a road known as The Croft.

3. Turn right and, when the road forks, continue ahead on a narrow lane. In a few metres, take a footpath on the right. Cross a drive and continue along the coast path to reach a junction of paths. The right-hand path descends to the beach at Waterwynch Bay.

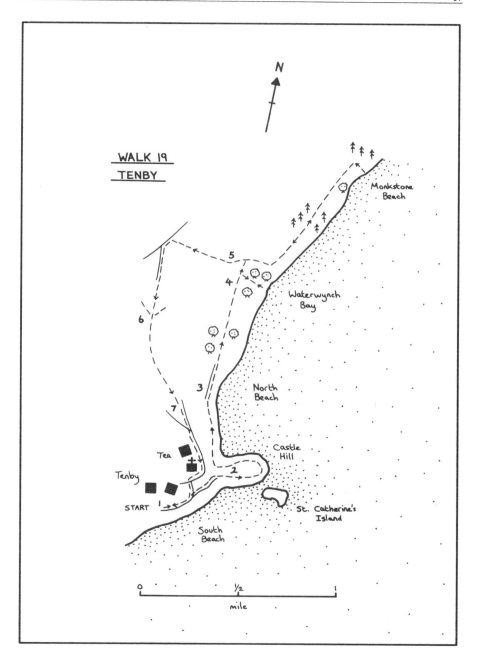

WALK 19
TENBY

4. The walk bears left to an access lane. If following the short route, skip all the directions before point 5. To continue on the longer walk, cross the lane and follow the coast path through woodlands. Go over a stream, and bear right uphill to enter a field. On reaching a fence, veer left and walk uphill. After crossing a number of stiles, descend into Lodge Valley. Follow the steep path out of the valley and above Monkstone Beach to a path junction. Take the first path on the right if you wish to visit the beach. To continue on the walk, retrace your steps to the access lane.

5. Follow the lane uphill to the A478. Turn left for about 50 metres then bear left along a lane. In approximately 300 metres go through a kissing gate on the right. Veer left to follow a clear path behind houses. On reaching the bottom corner of the field, go through a kissing gate and bear right to a path junction.

6. Ignore a path into a field, but turn left to follow an enclosed path between trees. Emerge on a road and bear left a few metres. Turn left on another path and descend through trees to emerge on the drive to the Aquarium. Walk downhill to a lane junction and turn right to the A478.

7. Turn left and pass The Croft on the left. Follow the road above the cliffs and ignore a lane on the left. Pass the Market Hall and the Upper Crust Tea Room on your right. Pass St Mary's Church and bear right into Church Street. Turn right again and go through the Five Arches. Turn left and, shortly, rejoin the outward route. Retrace your steps along the Esplanade to the start of the walk at the car park.

20. Manorbier

Route: Lanes, tracks and field paths lead to a fairly level stretch of the Pembrokeshire Coast path and exhilarating views. Children must be closely supervised on the cliff path.

Distance: 3 miles.

How to get there: Manorbier is on the B4585, about a mile off the A4139, west of Tenby and east of Pembroke.

Public Transport: Buses from Tenby and Haverfordwest pass through the village. Swansea - Pembroke trains stop at Manorbier station, which lies 1¼ miles north of the village.

Start: Manorbier beach car park, which is located below the castle.

Map: Outdoor Leisure 36.

Manorbier is a charming village with a castle and popular beach. The de Barri family built a fortress here in the 12th century, and parts of the present castle date from then. The famous Giraldus Cambrenis, also known as Gerald of Wales, was born in the castle about 1146. He was Norman on his father's side, but Welsh through his mother Anghared, the

Manorbier Castle and Bay

daughter of Nest. He studied at the Benedictine Abbey of St Peter in Gloucester and later went to Paris. He became Archdeacon of Brecon and in 1188 made a journey through Wales with Baldwin, the Archbishop of Canterbury to find recruits for the Third Crusade. His experiences can be read in his book titled 'The Journey through Wales'. Gerald hoped to become Bishop of St David's, but, despite a long struggle, he did not gain the bishopric because his ambition was also to free the Church in Wales from Canterbury. His later years were spent writing and he produced 17 books before he died in 1223. He had a great affection for Manorbier and called it 'the pleasantest spot in Wales'. The castle is open to visitors from Easter to the end of October from 10.30am - 5.30pm. There is an admission charge. Also of interest is the well-preserved medieval dovecote that can be reached by following a track that is almost opposite the car park for approximately 150 metres. The ruined mill is passed on the way.

The Tea Shop

The Chives Tea Rooms are situated in the heart of the village, and seating includes outdoor tables. There is a good selection of hot and cold dishes, including vegetarian meals, salads, sandwiches and cakes. Open from about Easter to the end of September. 9-30am - 5-00pm seven days a week. Shorter hours at the beginning and end of the season. Tel: 01834 871709.

The Walk

1. From the car park, walk out to the lane and turn right to pass below the castle, which is on your left. Ignore a lane leading to the church. On reaching a junction, bear right and, in about 20 metres, turn right along a lane. It eventually becomes unsurfaced.

2. On reaching a fork, turn left and pass a house on the left. Continue ahead and cross a stile. Bear right to pass through a gap where there was once a gate. Walk uphill to a stile and then through a gap in a hedge to arrive at a stile in front of a barn at Hill Farm.

3. Bear left on a track that soon bends right to pass farm buildings on the right. Emerge in a field and cross it to reach the opposite

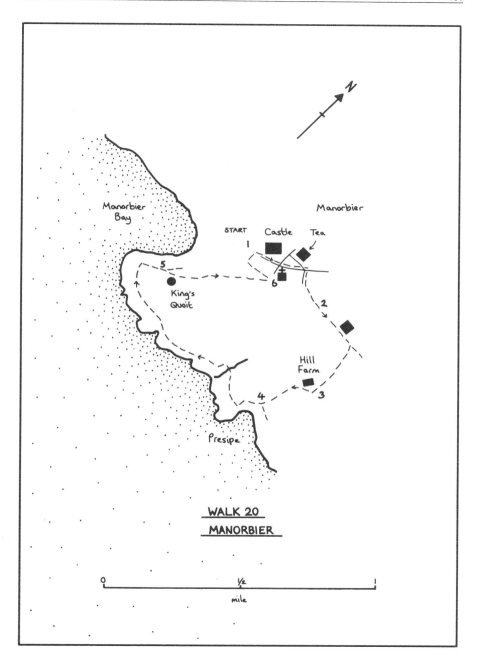

Manorbier Bay

Manorbier

START

Castle

Tea

1

5

6

King's Quoit

2

Hill Farm

4

3

Presipe

WALK 20
MANORBIER

0   ½   1
mile

fence. Turn left to have the fence on your right and cross a stile in the right-hand corner. Walk downhill towards the cliffs above Presipe beach.

4. Bear right to cross a stile and follow the coast path. In about 100 metres, a steep, stepped path descends to Presipe beach. The coast path continues above and around the cove then bears right above the valley called Coomb. Cross a stream and, on reaching a fork, it is advisable to take the higher path. Traverse around another cleft in the cliffs and descend slightly to pass above low cliffs. After rounding the point known as Priest's Nose, you will see the beach at Manorbier ahead. Continue along the coast path until you reach the stones of a burial chamber on your right.

> Known as King's Quoit, the Neolithic burial chamber lies in a spectacular position on the cliffs above Manorbier Bay. It is quite a low tomb and has a capstone roughly 4½ metres long and 2½ metres wide.

5. At the burial chamber, take a path on the right. At another fork, go left. After a stile, go through a broad gate. Pass a cemetery and bear left at the churchyard to reach the gate that gives access to St James church.

> St James church dates from the building of the original castle. Whilst the nave is 12th century, the transepts date from the 13th, and other parts have been added or altered since. In the chancel there is a 13th century effigy.

6. Follow the church drive. In about 50 metres a path on the left descends to the coast path. Go right to the car park. Alternatively, to go directly to the tea room, follow the drive to the lane and turn right. At the junction, bear right again.

21. Stackpole Quay

Route: A delightful walk following cliff paths, beaches, lakeside paths and tracks.

Distance: 6½ miles.

How to get there: Stackpole Quay is situated on the coast south of Pembroke. It may be approached from the B4319 road to Angle by turning off to go through Cheriton or Stackpole Elidor. Alternatively, leave the A4139 at Lamphey by taking the B4584 to Freshwater East and minor roads from there.

Public Transport: Infrequent buses from Pembroke to Bosherton and Stackpole village (off route) on schooldays only.

Start: Car park at Stackpole Quay.

Map: Outdoor Leisure 36.

The name Stackpole is thought to come from the Norse 'stac', meaning an isolated rock, and 'pollr', a small inlet. The Stackpole estate came to the Campbells of Cawdor early in the 18th century when heiress Elizabeth Lort married Sir Alexander Campbell. In 1735, the mansion Stackpole Court was built on the earlier Norman site. It was demolished in 1967 and the estate is now a National Trust property. The church in the hamlet of Stackpole Elidor contains some fine monuments and effigies. Local limestone used to be exported from Stackpole Quay.

The Tea Shop

The Boathouse Tearoom is situated adjacent to the coastal path, near the tiny harbour at Stackpole Quay. Walkers are very welcome and refreshments may be taken in the tearoom or at tables in the courtyard. The varied menu includes a Ramblers Lunch, Welsh Rarebit, salads, sandwiches and baguettes. The tearoom is well known for its cream teas. There is a fine selection of home-made cakes, including cheesecakes. Open 10.30am - 5.30pm. Open weekends only in March, then daily from April to the end of October. Tel: 01646 672058.

Cliffs near Stackpole Head

The Walk

1. From the car park, walk towards the sea. Pass the Boathouse Tearoom and turn right to go up some steps. At a path junction, continue up the stepped path to emerge on the headland. Follow the clear path ahead and descend the steps to the beach at Barafundle Bay.

2. Cross the beach to steps below the woodland on the opposite side of the bay. The path rises gradually onto the cliffs. Continue around the sheer cliffs, passing Stackpole Head, a number of 'blow-holes' and Saddle Point.

    Much of the coastline here drops sheer to the sea. At the base of the Cliffs are caves and isolated rocks. Look out for chough, fulmar, razorbill, guillemot and kittiwake as you walk along the high cliffs. The dunes of Stackpole Warren supported hundreds of generations of rabbits for the Cawdor Estate.

3. On reaching the sandy beach of Broad Haven, follow the stream (it may be dry) to a small bridge below cliffs. Cross an older

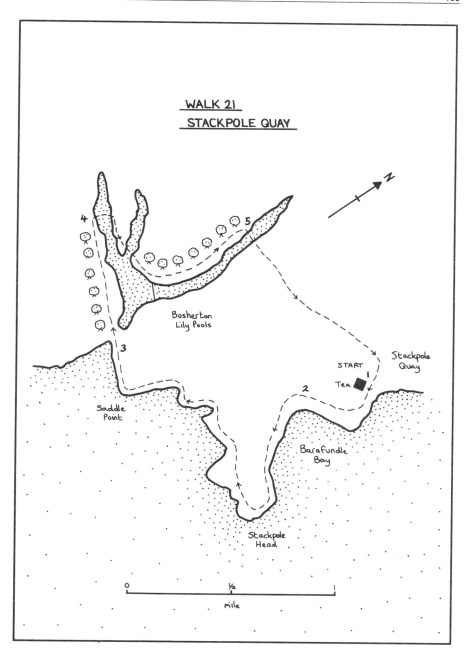

WALK 21
STACKPOLE QUAY

bridge and follow the path alongside Bosherton lily ponds. Cross a plank bridge and turn right at a path junction. After passing the Pump House, turn right again at the next junction.

Bosherton Lakes are at their best in May and June when parts of the ponds are covered with the flowers of white water lilies. The ponds were made in the late 18th and early 19th centuries after three narrow limestone valleys were dammed. Two had been tidal. The spurs between the lakes are covered with scrub. Birdwatchers should visit in winter, when wildfowl may be present.

4. Cross a walkway to the other side of the lily pond. Continue along the path to have the pond on your right. The path bears left then crosses a grassy area before descending to another walkway. Cross it and walk uphill to a signpost that says Middle Arm. Turn right to an old bridge known as Grassy Bridge. Do not cross it, but continue in the direction of Eastern Arm. The lily pond is still on your right.

5. On reaching the ancient bridge known as the Eight-Arched Bridge, cross it and go through a gate. This is a permissive route, which will return you to the car park. Follow the track ahead. There are a number of stiles placed next to the gates across the track. On reaching a track junction, continue ahead. After crossing another stile, you will emerge at the start of the walk in the car park.

22. Little Haven

Route: A lovely, varied walk that includes woodlands, lanes and cliff paths with superb coastal views. Children must be kept under control on the cliffs.

Distance: 6 miles.

How to get there: Little Haven is half a mile south of Broad Haven, which is on the B4341 west of Haverfordwest.

Public Transport: Buses from Haverfordwest to Broad Haven. A less frequent service to Little Haven.

Start: Little Haven car park.

Map: Outdoor Leisure 36.

Little Haven's picturesque, natural harbour was at one time a busy coal port. There were several pits in the area, both inland and along the cliffs. Coal was loaded directly from the beach to the boat. Nowadays, the beach is popular with families and sunbathers. At low tide, the beach links with the sands at Broad Haven.

Little Haven

The Tea Shop

The Post Office Tea Room at Little Haven is situated close to the little harbour and beach. Hot and cold drinks are available and a variety of snacks including jacket potatoes, sandwiches and home-made cakes and pastries. Open 9.00am - 5.00pm from Easter to October. Tel: 01437 781233.

The Walk

1. From the car park, turn right towards the sea. Bear right to cross the bridge over the stream. At a road junction, turn left uphill to follow the road in the direction of Broad Haven.

2. On reaching Broad Haven, walk along the sea front. Continue ahead when the road bends right. In about 100 metres, bear right on a footpath to the car park. From the middle bay, veer left to a footpath signposted to the Woodland Walk.

3. Follow the footpath to a fork. Go left to have a fence on the left and pass through a kissing gate. Cross a track and go through a similar gate. In approximately 100 metres, cross a stream and climb a boarded path through Haroldston Wood. The path becomes level for some distance and, in places, passes close to the stream, before climbing again. On reaching a three-way sign-post, ignore the left-hand path.

4. Pass a seat and viewpoint on the right. In another 150 metres, pass a timber chalet park. Continue on the main path and walk uphill through woodland. On reaching a path junction below a church, bear left to a stile near a gate.

5. Bear right to pass the Parish Church of Haroldston West. Ignore a lane on the right and continue ahead. In approximately 400 metres, turn left on a narrow lane signposted to Druidston Haven. It bends to the right.

    This stretch of lane is on the line of a prehistoric (Neolithic or Bronze Age) track that linked Monk Haven (St Ishmael's) and Whitesand (St David's). The trackway formed a safer route than the sea voyage around the dangerous rocky coast.

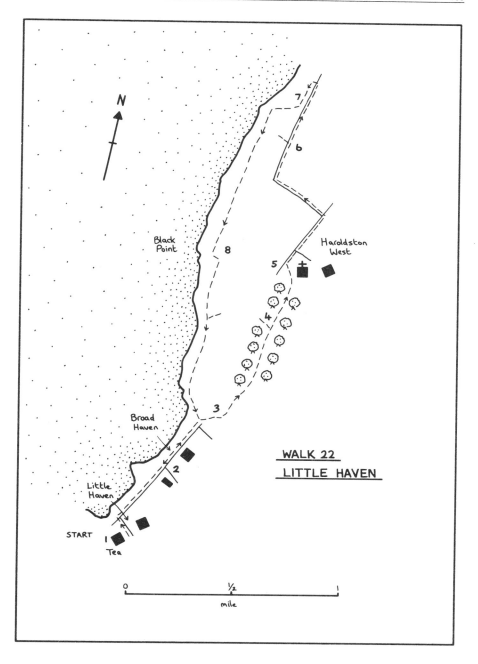

N

Black
Point

8

7

6

Haroldston
West

5

4

Broad
Haven

3

2

Little
Haven

START

1

Tea

WALK 22
LITTLE HAVEN

0   ½   1
mile

6. On reaching a cattle grid, ignore the path on the left to Haroldston Chins, but continue along the lane to have views of Druidston Haven. About 500 metres beyond the cattle grid, turn left to follow the Pembrokeshire Coast Path.

    From the coast path you can enjoy superb views of St Bride's Bay. St Bride (also called Bridget and, in Wales, Ffraid) founded a monastery at Kildare in AD490. Although she never left Ireland, several places in Wales are named after her. Her cult spread to Cornwall and Brittany. There are several isolated stacks to look out for along this stretch of coastline. The Iron Age fort near Black Point is slipping into the sea. In spring and summer, masses of wild flowers flourish on the cliffs.

7. The path passes below a section of road previously walked before it bears right towards the cliffs. Walk up to a stile and follow a clear path along the cliff top. Pass the viewpoint above Haroldston Chins and, in another kilometre, the natural arch called Haroldston Bridge.

8. Pass the Iron Age hill fort at Black Point and, farther on, ignore a path on the left. Follow the coast path as it gradually descends to Broad Haven. Retrace your steps to the start. At low tide, it may be possible to return to Little Haven by walking along the beach.

23. St David's

Route: A fairly easy walk along field and cliff paths amongst superb coastal scenery.

Distance: 3½ miles.

How to get there: St David's is on the A487 between Haverfordwest and Fishguard.

Public Transport: Buses from Fishguard and Haverfordwest.

Start: Cross Square in the centre of St David's.

Map: Outdoor Leisure 35.

St David, the patron saint of Wales, founded a monastery here in the 6th century. It survived the Viking raids but when the Normans came, they imposed their own form of monasticism and appointed a royal official as bishop. The church was consecrated as a cathedral in 1131. Two journeys to St David's were considered equal to one pilgrimage to Rome. The cathedral became rich and a new church was built which, in later centuries, had chapels added to the main structure. In the early 14th century, Bishop Gower made several changes including the south porch and the rood screen. Later, the Norman roof was replaced with an oak ceiling. Restoration work was carried out by John Nash about 1800, and later by Gilbert Scott. Built between 1280 and 1350, the Bishop's Palace is a magnificent ruin. In Cross Square stands a medieval preaching cross.

The Tea Shop

The cosy Iron Kettle Tea Room is situated close to Cross Square. A variety of snacks is available including baked potatoes and Cawl (a traditional Welsh vegetable soup). Cream teas, bara brith, Welsh cakes and a selection of home-made cakes are on offer. Open daily 9.00am - 5.30pm Easter to late October.

The Walk

1.   From Cross Square, take the road that goes in the direction of St Justinian and Porth Clais. In about 30 metres, turn left. At the next junction, turn left again. Take the next road on the right and pass some bungalows.

2. On reaching a track, turn right for approximately 50 metres, and then bear left along an enclosed path. Cross a stile and continue beside a left-hand hedge. The clear path crosses a number of stiles before emerging on the coast path above St Non's Bay. Turn right along it, but leave immediately by taking a path on the right to St Non's Well.

> Situated close to St Non's Chapel, St Non's Well was regarded as a healing well for hundreds of years, and was visited long after the chapel fell out of use. It was said to ebb and flow with the tide. The waters were reputed to cure all kinds of ailments and children were regularly brought here to bathe. On St Non's Day, 2nd March, offerings of pins were placed in the well. The stone vault over it was built in the 18th century.

St Non's Well

3. Go through a kissing gate to St Non's Chapel.

> Non was St David's mother and, according to legend, he was born on the site of the chapel during a thunderstorm. At the time, she was being pursued by David's father King Sant (of Cardigan). The

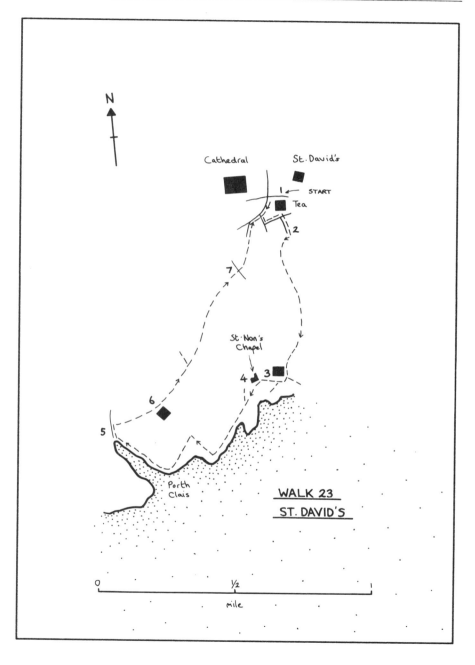

N

Cathedral   St. David's

1 ← START

Tea

2

7

St. Non's
Chapel

4 3

6

5

Porth
Clais

WALK 23
ST. DAVID'S

0   ½   1

mile

date of the chapel is uncertain, although it is known there was a chapel here in the early 1300s. The incised stone standing against a corner is thought to be 7th - 9th century.

4. From the chapel, take a clear path to a stone stile and the coast path. Turn right and follow the cliff path alongside dramatic cliff scenery to the harbour at Porth Clais.

St David was baptised at a spring north of Porthclais harbour by St Eilbyn (St Elvis), an Irish bishop. The breakwater at the end of the creek may date from Norman times. It was repaired in the 18th century. Porthclais was the harbour for St David's and coal, limestone and timber were landed here. Restored limekilns are on the quays. Coal was imported until the 1950s for the local gasworks.

5. Do not cross the bridge, but turn right along the lane. Almost immediately, leave it to bear right on a path, uphill. On reaching a field, walk straight across it to a gate. Follow the left-hand hedge through the next field towards a farm. Turn left on the farm access track and, in a few paces, cross a stile on the right.

6. Walk straight ahead along the right side of the field. Cross a stile and maintain your direction to a kissing gate and enclosed track. Ignore a ladder stile on the left and walk ahead along the track. Pass a seat and, in another 100 metres, emerge on a lane.

7. Cross the lane and continue ahead. In a few metres, turn left on another track. When it ends, follow a road around a bend to a junction. Turn right to return to the start of the walk at Cross Square.

24. Goodwick

Route: A fairly energetic walk that is rewarded with superb coastal views. Cliff and field paths with some road and lane walking. Children must be closely supervised on the coast path.

Distance: 7 miles.

How to get there: Goodwick is on the A487, west of Fishguard.

Public Transport: Trains to Fishguard harbour, ¾ mile from the start. Buses from St David's, Haverfordwest and Cardigan to Fishguard town centre, 1¼ miles from the start. Buses from Fishguard to Goodwick.

Start: Car park near the roundabout, harbour and Ocean Lab.

Map: Outdoor Leisure 35.

Goodwick was a small fishing village before the building of the North Breakwater, railway station and quay. It was expected that transatlantic liners would call at Fishguard and their passengers would travel on to London by train. This trade only lasted a few years until the outbreak of the First World War. It is now exclusively an Irish ferry terminal.

The Tea Shop

The Ocean Lab Café is in a modern glass building on the Parrog near the harbour and the East Breakwater. The Tourist Information Centre is in the same building, as well as the Ocean Lab, a gift shop and cyber café. Home-made refreshments are on offer, including soup, sandwiches, bara brith, scones, apple pie and cream. Open 10.00am - 6.00pm Easter to October.

The Walk

1. From the car park, walk out to the roundabout and take the road uphill towards Goodwick town centre. On reaching a road junction, bear left. In a few metres, turn right on a road called New Hill. Walk uphill and, at a junction where car parking is signposted on the left, take the right fork through an estate called Harbour Village.

2. At the end of the road there are seats overlooking the harbour.

With the sea on your right, continue ahead on the coast path. After going downhill and rising again, the path crosses a stream and rises to a stile on the left. Cross it and go through a gap. Bear right to pass through gorse. On reaching a field, go diagonally left to follow a wall and fence to another stile. Pass above Anglais Bay and Porth Maen.

3. Continue on the undulating coastal path. It climbs between outcrops, heather and gorse. Ignore a narrow path on the left and walk uphill before descending to cross streams above Pant y Dwr.

4. The path rises above another small inlet before passing around Aber Felin Bay. Cross a stile and follow a fence on the left to another stile. In about 30 metres you will see a stile on the left. The route leaves the coast here, but, if you have the energy, it is worthwhile to make the diversion to Carregwastad Point. Follow the coast path downhill into a valley. Cross a footbridge over a stream and climb a stepped path before bearing right to the monument on Carregwastad Point.

Monument on Carregwastad Point

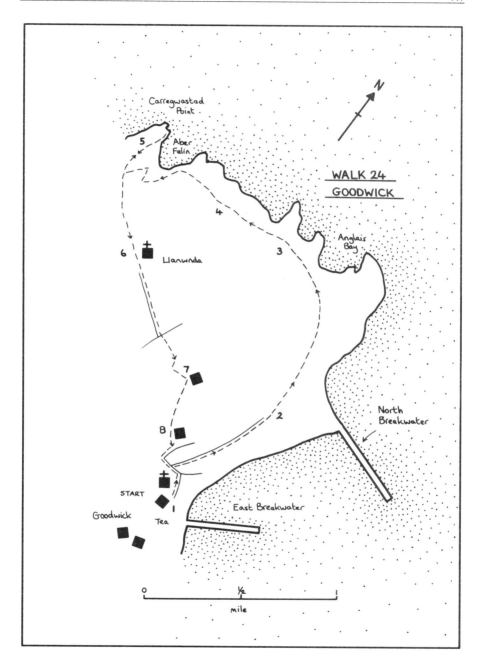

WALK 24
GOODWICK

At Carregwastad a French expeditionary force of mainly ex-convicts landed on the 22 February 1797 under the command of an American called Tate. The French had hopes that their force of 1200 could start an uprising amongst the peasants against the English. They intended to sail up the Bristol Channel but the winds prevented them from doing this and, after being sighted at St David's and Fishguard, they came ashore at Carregwastad. The men were soon drunk on Portuguese wine local people had recovered from a recent shipwreck. They started to advance towards Goodwick but by then Lord Cawdor and the local militia were ready to attack. Local legend says that Welsh countrywomen in red cloaks and hats who had congregated to watch were mistaken by the French for soldiers. One woman, Jemina Nicholas, rounded up several Frenchmen with her pitchfork. Tate realised his men were in no condition to fight, and the surrender was signed in the Royal Oak in Fishguard on the 24 February 1797. The memorial stone on Carregwastad Point was erected in 1897 to commemorate the event.

5. Return the way you came by crossing the footbridge to reach the path going inland. Cross the stile and, in a few metres, slant left to enter another field. Maintain your direction to follow the left side of this field. Cross a stile near a gate. Walk across the field to a broad gate and follow a grassy track to a stile. Cross the field by slanting right towards the right side of the church seen across the fields. Cross a stile near a gate and follow the track ahead. It bends to the left. On reaching buildings, bear right. Pass Llanwnda church on your left.

The small church at Llanwnda is dedicated to the 6th century Breton saint, St Gwyndaf. Although restored in the 19th century, the building retains its medieval roof beams. On the outside walls are five inscribed stones.

6. Walk ahead along the lane. Pass a rocky hill on the right. Ignore a track on the right and bear left with the lane to pass a cemetery. On reaching a lane junction, cross directly over to a track. Ignore a track to Anfield on the right. Pass stables and continue on an enclosed track. Ignore a path on the right and follow the track as it bears left, and right, downhill. Emerge near farm buildings.

7. Turn right and ignore a gate that gives access to the farmyard. Continue ahead on the track, which becomes grassy and narrow. On reaching a junction of paths, stay on the main path.

8. On reaching a house and lane, turn right, downhill. Follow the lane around a left bend, to have a stream on the right. Ignore a footbridge across the stream. Continue along the lane. At a junction, bear right to the next junction, in Goodwick. Turn left and ignore a road on the right. In another 40 metres, turn right to retrace your steps to the roundabout and start of the walk.

25. Cilgerran

Route: Woodland paths above and through the spectacular Teifi gorge lead to the Welsh Wildlife Centre in the Teifi marshes. Some paths can be slippery after rain. Easy level paths and tracks are used for the return to Cilgerran.

Distance: 4½ miles.

How to get there: Cilgerran is off the A478, south of Cardigan.

Public Transport: Cilgerran is on the infrequent Cardigan to Crymych bus route. Cardigan-Tenby bus route on the A478, 1¼ miles from the start. The roundabout south of Cardigan can be reached by public footpath from the nature reserve.

Start: Car park near the river in Cilgerran.

Map: Outdoor Leisure 35.

Cilgerran is known for its ruined medieval castle that stands on a precipitous cliff overlooking the dramatic Teifi gorge. Little is known of its early history but it may be the castle from which Nest, wife of the Norman lord Gerald de Windsor, was abducted by Owain ap Cadwgan. Lord Rhys captured the stronghold in 1164 but forty years later it was regained by the Normans, only to be recaptured by the Welsh in 1215. Eight years later, the castle was in Norman hands again and they began to rebuild it. The ruins we see today date from that period. Owain Glyndŵr's troops held Cilgerran for a short period in 1405. During the reign of Henry VIII, the castle was given to the Vaughan family and they occupied it until the early 17th century. Uncared for, the castle became a romantic ruin, much visited by tourists and artists. Turner made four paintings of it c1825-8.

The Tea Shop

The Nuthatch Restaurant and Tea Room is located on the upper floor of the Welsh Wildlife Centre. A selection of main meals, salads, baguettes, sandwiches and homebaked cakes are available. Open 10.30am - 4.30pm every day from Easter to October.

The Walk

1.   From the car park, turn left to walk along with the river on your right. Shortly after passing the end of a building, bear left up steps. Pass the castle on your right and walk out to a lane. Turn right and, in approximately 120 metres, bear right on a track.

2. Descend to cross a footbridge over the river Plysgog. Walk uphill past cottages to emerge on a track. Bear left to pass a house and, in about 50 metres, cross a stile on the right. Walk ahead across the field beside the right-hand hedge and enter a wood. Follow a clear path through the trees. After crossing a couple of plank bridges, the path goes uphill and continues along the edge of the wood.

3. On reaching a stile on the left, just beyond farm buildings, cross it and turn right. In about 200 metres, go through a gate and walk ahead to a stile on the right. Take care as you follow the path to the right, high above the river. It is stepped in places but can be slippery after rain. Descend gradually through woodland to the River Teifi and the nature reserve. Walk ahead on a better path to have the river on your right. Ignore a signpost for the Squirrel Trail on your left and emerge on a wider path. Bear left to the Wildlife Centre and Nuthatch Restaurant.

The River Teifi

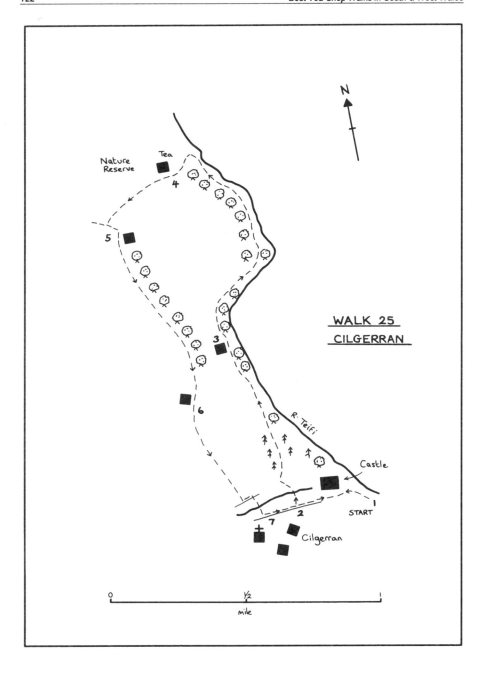

The Teifi Marshes Nature Reserve is considered one of the finest wetland reserves in Wales. It encompasses a variety of habitats including woodland, water meadows and reed swamp. Many kinds of birds visit the reserve and there are occasional sightings of uncommon species such as ruff, little egret and marsh harrier. Cetti's warblers are present all year. Otters are seen regularly on the River Teifi. Water buffalo have been brought into the swamp to improve the reedbed habitat for wildfowl. The Visitor Centre has wildlife and other exhibitions. The tea room is open to public footpath walkers, but enquire at the reception if you wish to explore the reserve's other paths as there may be a charge.

4. Return to the main track and follow it to the Visitor Centre car park. On reaching it, veer left on the main track and, in about 200 metres, where there is a footpath on the right for the Otter Hide, turn left on a track. Ignore the Squirrel Trail on the left and walk ahead to pass a house. Continue ahead to a path junction.

5. Turn right and follow the clear path along the edge of woodland to a stile. Continue on the path with fields nearby on the right and pass old quarry workings on the left. Join a wider path and walk ahead to pass a bungalow on the right. Emerge on a track and turn right.

6. Follow the track as it bends to the left and go through a gate across it. Pass buildings on the left and continue ahead through another gate to emerge on a lane. Turn left and veer right almost immediately to walk downhill between houses. Cross a footbridge over the river Plysgog and walk uphill to a lane. Turn left and pass the church of St Llawddog on your right.

St Llawddog was a Welsh monk who lived in the 6th century. The church dates from the 13th century but it was extensively rebuilt in the mid-19th century. In the churchyard, on the south side of the church, there is a 6th century stone engraved in Latin and Ogham to mark the grave of Tregennussus, son of Macutrenus.

7. Continue along the lane to rejoin your outward route. Retrace your steps to the castle and start of the walk.

Also of Interest:

BEST TEA SHOP WALKS IN SNOWDONIA

Dorothy Hamilton

Enjoy a leisurely ramble in beautiful Snowdonia and complete the experience with afternoon tea at a recommended tea room! Visiting both popular and lesser-known areas, these 27 circular walks range from three and a half to eight miles. You can walk Conwy mountain, explore Gwydr Forest and its lakes, or walk in the Lledr and Ffestiniog valleys. The author's clear directions are accompanied by sketch maps, photographs and notes on local history and wildlife. £6.95

BEST TEA SHOP WALKS IN THE CLWYDIAN HILLS AND WELSH BORDERLANDS

Dorothy Hamilton

25 mostly circular walks from 3 to 10 miles through the Clwydian Hills, particularly appealing to families. Climb the highest peak of the Clwydian range, visit the spectacular Eglwyseg escarpment or stroll through gentler countryside in the Vale of Clwyd or Glyn Ceiriog. Several routes explore sections of the Offa's Dyke path. Clear directions, sketch maps and photographs are accompanied by notes on local history and wildlife. Teashops are found in National Trust properties, a former workhouse and a garden centre. £6.95

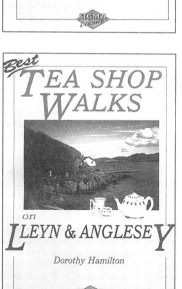

BEST TEA SHOP WALKS: LLEYN & ANGLESEY

Dorothy Hamilton

Leisurely walks to enjoy, not endure, and all with the promise of a delicious afternoon tea!

The routes range from 3 to 8 miles, will suit all ages and experience, and cover a vast variety of scenery. There's the opportunity to explore magnificent cliff scenery, enjoy dramatic views of offshore islands, visit picturesque coastal hamlets and remote valleys. To replenish your energy levels, each route includes a 'tea shop stop' personally recommended by the author, and to feed your mind there's notes on local history and wildlife. £6.95

NORTH WALES WALKS ON THE LEVEL - Snowdonia & Anglesey

Norman Buckley

25 circular walks in the hills and mountains of North Wales, intended for those who enjoy gentle walking in fine surroundings but do not wish to make significant ascents. Route maps, descriptions of towns and villages, landscape and interesting features are all included. There is a summary of each walk, including length and total ascent. £6.95

BEST PUB WALKS IN SNOWDONIA

Laurence Main

A strenuous hike up Snowdon, or a leisurely amble in the foothills. There's a huge variety here, with the assurance of a welcome in the hillsides for weary walkers. £6.95

SNOWDONIA WALKS WITH CHILDREN

Nick Lambert

These 20, circular walks have been chosen and written with children in mind, and cover the whole of Snowdonia, taking in a wide variety of the national park's scenery. Some routes feature well-known beauty spots, others explore quieter, lesser-frequented areas where it is possible to 'get away from it all' and enjoy the peace of the countryside. £6.95

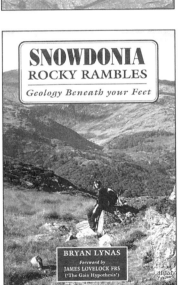

SNOWDONIA ROCKY RAMBLES: Geology Beneath your Feet

Bryan Lynas

This sequel to Lakeland Rocky Rambles, with a Foreword by James Lovelock FRS, is much more than a book of mountain walks. Each of the ten is a voyage of discovery and a journey through time, with insights into the geology, wildlife and history of these splendid peaks. £9.95

All of our books are available through booksellers. In case of difficulty, or for a free catalogue, please contact: **SIGMA LEISURE, 1 SOUTH OAK LANE, WILMSLOW, CHESHIRE SK9 6AR.** Phone: 01625-531035 Fax: 01625-536800. E-mail: info@sigmapress.co.uk Web site: http//www.sigmapress.co.uk

MASTERCARD and VISA orders welcome.